PHILOSOPHICAL ESSAYS

MAXIMS

"If you talk non-sense in Saxon, you are found out at once."
Walter Raleigh

"Man is an analogy drawing animal; that is his great good fortune.
His danger is of treating analogies as identities . . . ."
H. W. Auden. *The Dyer's Hand*

MINIM

"Will you walk into my parlor," said the Philosopher* to the fly.
Mary Howitt

*Misprint

Philosophical Essays

O. K. BOUWSMA

UNIVERSITY OF NEBRASKA PRESS · LINCOLN

Manufactured in the United States of America

PREFACE

ALL THE ESSAYS in this book except the last one have been published before. They are collected now with permission. The first, "Moore's Theory of Sense-Data," was published in *The Philosophy of G. E. Moore*, Volume IV of The Library of Living Philosophers, edited by Paul Arthur Schilpp, now published by The Open Court Publishing Co., LaSalle, Illinois.

"The Expression Theory of Art" was published in a volume called *Philosophical Analysis* edited by Max Black, now owned by Prentice-Hall.

The others were published in journals: "Descartes' Skepticism of the Senses in Mind," "Variations on a Theme by Mr. Costello," "Naturalism," "The Mystery of Time," and "The Blue Book" in the *Journal of Philosophy*; "Descartes' Evil Genius" and "Reflections on Moore's Recent Book" in *The Philosophical Review*; "On Many Occasions I Have in Sleep Been Deceived" in *Proceedings and Addresses of The American Philosophical Association*, 1957. The last, "The Terms of Ordinary Language Are...," was read as a paper in a symposium at a meeting of the Western Division of The American Philosophical Association.

I have long hesitated to assume the risk of the incalculable harm these essays might do but now in view of the likewise incalculable good they might do, I have tossed a coin and it came down just as I thought it would. It stood on its edge. And I knocked it down.

O. K. BOUWSMA

CONTENTS

PHILOSOPHICAL ESSAYS

MOORE'S THEORY OF SENSE-DATA

I

I WANT IN THIS ESSAY to discuss a few sentences from Professor
Moore's "A Defence of Common Sense," published in the
volume containing the second series of contributions to
Contemporary British Philosophy. These sentences are contained
in part IV of that contribution. In this part Professor Moore is
expounding what he regards as the correct analysis of such
sentences as "This is a hand," "That is the sun," "This is a
dog," etc. Involved in this exposition is the assertion: "whenever
I know or judge such a proposition to be true, there is always
some sense-datum about which the proposition in question is a
proposition—some sense-datum which is a subject of the
proposition in question." [1] Professor Moore goes on to recognize
"that some philosophers have...doubted whether there are
any such things as other philosophers have meant by 'sense-
data'," [2] and in order to make sure that his readers may be
persuaded, he goes on with the following attempt at definition,
which I quote.

Professor Moore writes:

And in order to point out to the reader what sort of things I
mean by sense-data, I need only ask him to look at his own

[1] J. H. Muirhead, ed., *Contemporary British Philosophy*, Second
Series (New York: Macmillan, 1924), p. 217.
[2] *Ibid.*, p. 217.

right hand. If he does this he will be able to pick out something (and unless he is seeing double, only one thing) with regard to which he will see that it is, at first sight, a natural view to take, that that thing is identical, not indeed, with his whole right hand, but with that part of its surface which he is actually seeing, but will also (on a little reflection) be able to see that it is doubtful whether it can be identical with the part of the surface of his hand in question. Things *of the sort* (in a certain respect) of which this thing is, which he sees in looking at his hand, and with regard to which he can understand how some philosophers should have supposed it to be the part of the surface of his hand which he is seeing, while others have supposed that it can't be, are what I mean by sense-data. I therefore define the term in such a way that it is an open question whether the sense-datum which I now see in looking at my hand and which is a sense-datum of my hand, is or is not identical with that part of its surface which I am now actually seeing.[3]

I propose first to discuss some difficulties in this paragraph. Professor Moore invites his readers to pick out something, but his directions for doing this are not clear. Commonly if one is asked to pick out something, the something is described. Out of this bowl, pick out the red flower; out of this sheaf pick out the longest straw. We should all know how to follow these directions. But Professor Moore's directions are not like this. Apparently you simply pick out something; that is, as you are looking at your hand, and keeping your eye on your hand, you pick out something. Suppose you pick out your knuckles. Certainly that is something you can pick out. Well, is that the sort of thing Professor Moore intended that you should pick out? It is not. And this is the test which what you pick out must satisfy in order to meet Professor Moore's requirement. You must pick out something "with regard to which. . .it is, at first sight, a natural view to take, that that thing is identical with that

[3] *Ibid.*, p. 218.

part of its surface which (you are) actually seeing." So of course, the knuckles won't do. Even the surface of the knuckles won't do. What better could one do, than pick out the surface of the hand one is seeing? Certainly you can pick this out and it would be a natural view to take that that thing is identical with that part of the surface which you are actually seeing. This is a bit doubtful however, since you would scarcely be expected to pick out the whole of the surface which you are seeing, for picking out is selecting, and after selection there would be a remainder, which in this case there would not be. Furthermore if you do pick out the surface of the hand which you are seeing, could you then (on a little reflection) doubt that it is the surface of the hand you are seeing? For until you manage to do this too you would not have picked out what Professor Moore means by a sense-datum.

I confess that I am unable with these directions to attain the desired result. Looking at my hand I can pick out knuckles, finger-tips, nails, lines, veins, etc., but to none of them does the description which Professor Moore gives apply. If I pick out the knuckles, I am not seized with any doubts that they are the surface of my hand; and so with the finger-tips, nails, etc. And how I should ever be in a position to anticipate that what I do pick out would satisfy the given conditions I do not understand. I can see how if yesterday I had been asked to pick out my thumb, and then a little later doubted that what I had picked out was my thumb (for I had my fingers crossed in an unusual way) then today I might, remembering, pick out what yesterday it seemed very natural to take to be identical with my thumb and then what later I came to doubt was identical with my thumb. But Professor Moore's directions are not like this. He says that there is something which you may pick out and with respect to it, you will have the described difficulty. I have not been able to pick it out.

This, then, is one peculiarity of Professor Moore's directions. One who is unacquainted with sense-data, and so has no information with regard to what to pick out, must resort to random picking, and wish for luck. Professor Moore's directions are something like this: Pick out of this basket something of which you will see that it is, at first sight, a natural view to take that that thing is identical with a red marble, but of which you will also see that it is doubtful whether it can be identical with the red marble. Now one might look at the basket and notice what there is in it. Here is a red marble, here a red pepper, here a red rubber ball, etc. One might notice all these things, and turn away, saying that there was nothing there which seemed at first glance to be a red marble, and then a moment later seemed not to be a red marble. So there was nothing to pick out. On the other hand, there might be something red and round in that basket which did at first appear to be a red marble, and then upon closer inspection turned out to be a red rubber ball. And picking out the red rubber ball would satisfy the directions. I am trying by these analogies to figure out just what sort of directions these are that Professor Moore is giving, in order to show why I have been unable in looking at my hand to discover anything which I should have some reason to suppose met with Professor Moore's directions.

But this is a general comment. Professor Moore says that there is something about which you first feel sure and then about which you doubt. In seeking for this I do not see how in feeling sure one could anticipate the doubting. But I should like further to notice some peculiarities concerning what it is one is at first to be sure of, and then is to doubt. I have in mind Professor Moore's use of the following types of sentence, in which X symbolizes the something which you are able to pick out:

1. X is identical with the surface of my right hand.
2. X can be identical with the surface of my right hand.
3. X cannot be identical with the surface of my right hand.

I want first to consider the first type of sentence in order to make clear the context in which we should commonly understand it. And for this purpose I am going to define a certain word, parodying the definition which Moore gives of the word sense-datum. This is the parody:

"And in order to point out to the reader what sort of thing I mean by ———, I need only ask him to look at the cook's right hand. If he does this he will be able to pick out something with regard to which he will see that it is at first a natural view to take that that thing is identical not indeed with the cook's whole right hand, but with that part of its surface which one is actually (?) seeing but will also (on a little inspection) be able to see that it is doubtful whether it can be identical with the part of the hand in question. Things of the sort of which this thing is, which he sees in looking at the cook's hand, and with regard to which he can understand how some kitchen visitors should have supposed it to be the part of the surface of the cook's hand at which he was looking, while others have supposed that it can't be, are what I mean by rubber gloves."

This experiment, I think, might do very well for all kitchen visitors. But obviously its success depends upon a familiarity with the use of the expression "human hand" by which the inspection is guided. Look closely at the hand; does it look like a hand? pinch it, smell it, etc. Does the surface stretch like taffy, is it very smooth, etc.? Apparently in a case such as this there is no difficulty in distinguishing the surface of a hand from the surface of rubber gloves. Now then, when the reader in Professor Moore's experiment looks at his hand, and sees the surface of his hand, what happens? Does he think that some new kind of gloves, made to resemble the hand, have come to be worn, and that these gloves are, to smell, and touch, and sight, indistinguishable from the surface of the hand, gloves which you may not know you are wearing unless you remember that you put them on? If in a case of this sort one forgot, would one then be sensing, directly perceiving, a sense-datum? The answer is: No. For what distinguishes the doubt in terms of which Professor Moore defines the sense-datum, is that it cannot be resolved. Once the doubt arises, there is no way of settling the question whether the thing one can pick out is identical with the surface of one's hand or not. It must be remembered that Professor Moore does not say that the sense-datum is not identical with the surface of the hand. He only says that in looking at one's hand one comes to doubt that something, which may be the surface of one's hand, is the surface of one's hand. But, unlike the doubt about the surface of the hand and the rubber gloves, it cannot be settled. Once the doubt has arisen, there's nothing to do but to go on doubting. Scratching, smelling, looking more closely, do not give relief.

I can imagine someone in a facetious vein suggesting that the situation which Professor Moore describes is more like trying to distinguish identical twins occupying the same space. It's as though someone had been told: "He's identical twins," and then whenever that someone saw him, he would shake his head, looking, wondering, asking himself: Am I seeing Hans or Fritz? or when I am directly perceiving Hans, am I indirectly perceiving Fritz? He cannot decide. If someone says: You're seeing Hans, (that seems the natural view to take) he proceeds to doubt: "Maybe it's Fritz." He might in this situation easily come to see that some people would hold that Hans was not twins, and that Fritz is either an alternative notation for Fritz, or a meaningless expression.

Now I want to try a further experiment, again to exhibit the misleading familiarity of Professor Moore's language. In the experiment designed to test for rubber gloves, the point made was that Moore's language is applicable to such things as hands and gloves. I want now to show that it is also applicable to mirror-images. This is the experiment: "And in order to point out to the reader what I mean by ———, I need only ask him to look into the mirror, holding up his right hand to the glass. If he does this, he will be able to pick out something with regard to which he will see, that it is, at first sight, a natural view to take, that that thing is identical, not indeed with his whole right hand, but with that part of the surface which is reflected there, but will also (smiling to himself) be able to see that it is doubtful whether it can be identical with the part of the surface of his hand in question. Things of this sort of which this thing is, which he sees in looking at the reflection of his hand, and with regard to which he can understand how some creatures, little people and puppies, should have supposed it to be the part of the surface of his hand, while grown-ups supposed that it can't be, are what I mean by hand-mirror-images."

Now the point of these two analogous experiments is this: If you are among those philosophers who doubt that there are any such things as some philosophers have meant by sense-data, and if you try to understand Professor Moore's directions in the attempt to identify a sense-datum, then further if you interpret a philosopher's language as so much English, you are certain to fail. If you look at your hand and try to stir up doubts about what you are seeing, you may object to yourself: But maybe I am wearing rubber gloves. Well, you know how to take care of that. Or you may object: But maybe I am looking into a mirror, and what I see, is just an image. You also know how to take care of that. What other misgiving suggestion remains then? It must be remembered that Professor Moore says that the doubt arises "on a little reflection" though he does not, in this context at least, tell us at all what reflection induces the doubt. It won't do, of course, to object: But maybe there are sense-data, and it is a property of sense-data to pass for the surface of things we look at, both when and if they are, and when and if they are not, the surfaces of objects. For it is by means of some reflection which does not involve that there are sense-data, but that leads to the requisite doubt concerning the surface of one's hand, that one is persuaded that there are sense-data. What I mean to point out here is that the language of the experiment is strange language so long as we are not acquainted with sense-data. Once we distinguish a sense-datum we may come to see how it applies. But before we can do this we must come to doubt. And before we come to doubt we must indulge in a "little reflection." The question is: what reflection? What is it that led Professor Moore and some other philosophers to come to that pass where, when each looks at his hand, he may ask without the slightest perturbation: And is this the surface of a hand? If, actually seeing the surface of his hand, he says: "Maybe not," then he is aware of a sense-datum. The question is: What thoughts lead him to this doubt?

Before I go on to consider what these reflections may be, I

should like to discuss the second and third kinds of sentences above:

2. X can be identical with the surface of my right hand.
3. X cannot be identical with the surface of my right hand.

For this, notice a case of doubt in which one might have employed language of the sort which Professor Moore uses. Isaac on the day when he was deceived might have asked: Is this the hand of Jacob or the hand of Esau? Isaac was touching the hand and hearing the voice. The voice led him to doubt. We all understand this. And he might, had he attended Cambridge, have said: The hand that I am touching (and which I have picked out) is identical with the hand that is Esau's. I suppose that generally no one ever bothers to say a thing like this unless some doubt has preceded the assertion. So Isaac expected that this was the hand of Esau, but the voice made him doubtful. How could this be Esau's hand, when the voice which accompanied it sounded like Jacob's voice? In a dispute then, and to settle the matter (Isaac was very old!) Isaac may have said: This hand is identical with Esau's hand. He was wrong of course, but the confusion was one of hands; he mistook Jacob's hand for Esau's hand. The occasion for the use of the sentence arises after doubt and after denial. "What do you see?" "My right hand." "Oh, no you don't." "I say (temper rising) that what I see, is identical with my right hand. It is my right hand." It follows, of course, that we also have a use for: X is not identical with my right hand. If Rebecca on that occasion long ago, had had a mind to, she might have interrupted with: "You're wrong, Isaac. That hand is not identical with the hand of Esau. It's Jacob's hand."

Now we can also make a case for "This hand can be the hand of Esau," and so with "This hand cannot be the hand of Esau." Rebecca might have said: "It can't be." And then she would have given reasons, for such statements as "It can be" and "It can't be" have this sort of reference. So Isaac might have asked: Why can't it be? And the answer might have been: See here: You know that Esau's is a hairy hand. If you pull at the hairs on his hand, it pains him and you can see it on his face. And what is more the hair does not pull out. Try that experiment on this hand. There is no pain. The hair easily pulls off, and under the layer of hair, you will find paste. That's why this cannot be Esau's hand. Esau's hand is a genuine hairy, but this hand is a wolf's hand in sheep's clothing. To which Isaac might have lamented: But I thought it was Esau's. And it could have been for all I knew. The hand was hairy, it smelled of the field and of game, like Esau's hand. And it seemed like a large hand to me. So you see it could have been Esau's hand.

It is clearly, I think, situations such as these which we have in mind in the use of the expressions which Professor Moore employs. There is mistaking one thing for another thing, Jacob's hand for Esau's hand. There are also considerations which are involved in making the mistake, and other considerations which are involved in correcting the mistake. These considerations are of two kinds. If we are clear about what Jacob's hand is like, and clear about what Esau's hand is like, then the respects in which they are similar are likely to involve us in mistaking one for the other. The respects in which they are dissimilar, are the considerations which we draw upon when we correct our mistake, or when we come to say that "This cannot be so and so."

Accordingly, when Professor Moore says that you can pick out something about which you are inclined to say that it is identical with the surface of your hand, and this arises in a context in which you are inclined to say both that it can be, and that it cannot be, one would expect that some reasons would be at hand in respect to both. What makes you think that what you can pick out, can be identical with the surface of your hand and what makes you think that it cannot be identical with it? Is what you picked out similar in certain respects to the surface of your right hand, and dissimilar in certain other respects to that surface? Professor Moore has said that one would come to doubt by way of "a little reflection," as I noticed before, and the analysis which we have just made would lead one to expect that the reflection would consist in noticing similarities and dissimilarities between what you picked out and the surface of your right hand. Of course, if any dissimilarities were noticed, that ought to settle the matter. If the something is dissimilar, then of course, it is not the surface of one's hand. It looks as though one is aware of nothing but similarities, supposing one has picked out something, and yet that one is suspicious that there may be dissimilarities of which one is unaware. It's as though one were looking at one's hand, and had a suspicion that what one was seeing was not one's hand at all. So one examined one's hand carefully, found out that it was exactly what one expected one's hand to be like and yet concluded: "But maybe there is something I am not seeing, maybe there's a difference I am missing. So maybe after all, this is not my hand." What then planted this suspicion?

There is one further point that I should like to make. The experiment which Professor Moore proposes, takes for granted that each of us knows how to identify the surface of his hand. It is in terms of this identification that we are to come to recognize the something we pick out. Now then, each of us is able to describe his own hand. One might take a print of it, study it carefully for color shadings, shape and surface markings. If then one is well-informed about the surface of one's own hand, the doubt which Professor Moore describes does not arise because of any lack of information about one's hand. Apparently then the something which you pick out has the same characteristics which the surface of your hand has. If it did not have the same characteristics, obviously it would be different from the surface of your hand, and if it had the same and some others, it would also be different. So, if it has any characteristics at all, it must have the same characteristics as the surface of your hand. How then explain the suggestion that they are different? Are they in different places? This is also out of the question. We do not see the surface of the hand in one place, and pick out the something in a different place. If we did the doubt that the "something" and the surface of my hand are identical, would be settled. This too does not explain the suggestion that the something and the surface of my hand are identical. What then? If what I have just suggested about knowing the surface of one's hand is not admitted, then what? Then certainly we are at a loss. The experiment presupposes that we know something, and that by way of this we may become aware of something else. If you know the surface of your hand, you can become acquainted with your knuckles. You certainly can, if you look at your hand, pick out your knuckles. In some such way as this you also become acquainted with "a sense-datum." Suppose however that, in a situation in which you did pick out your knuckles, you were seized with a doubt as to whether your knuckles were identical with the surface of your right hand which you are seeing, how would you account for this? If nothing very serious has happened, one might suggest that you had now come to use the expression "the surface of my hand" in a very unusual way. I have an inkling that something of this sort has happened in the sentences from Professor Moore's exposition. If one can think that "the something which one can pick out" is identical with the surface of one's hand, then either one must take for granted the use of the expression "the surface of one's hand" which applies then to something one can see, smell, touch, kiss, etc., and so grant that what one can pick out is also something which one can see, smell, touch, kiss, etc., and otherwise one takes for granted the use of the expression "what one can pick out" knowing well what this is like that one can pick out, and that for instance one cannot touch, taste, smell, etc., what one can pick out, and so grant also that "the surface of my hand" is something which, like what one can pick out, can be seen, but cannot be touched, tasted, smelled, etc. Either, then, Professor Moore is in effect saying that you can pick out a physical object which is identical with the surface of your hand, or you can pick out something which is not a physical object at all, and that is identical with the surface of your hand. The puzzle is as to how a non-physical object (a sense-datum) can be identical with a physical object.

It seems at any rate inevitable that if anything can be conceived
to be the surface of my hand, it must be physical; and that if the
surface of my hand can be conceived to be a sense-datum, the
surface of my hand is not physical. But in that case what has
happened to the expression: "the surface of my hand?"

II

I have tried, in what preceded, to point out some of the
difficulties which I have met in trying to follow Professor
Moore's directions. And I regard as crucial in this respect the
three sentences which I discussed, and the use of the phrase:
"the surface of my hand." I also noticed that what leads to the
doubt in Professor Moore's experiment, is a "little reflection."
My suggestion is that it is the same "little reflection" which leads
us to use these sentences, and the phrase just noticed. And I
want now to describe the reflections which, in my own case,
seems to lead me in that direction.

There are especially three sets of facts which lead me to try
to distinguish a sense-datum in the prescribed way. One is
certain facts concerning sounds, odors and tastes. Another is
facts concerning mirror reflections, images, echoes, etc. And a
third is the use of such expressions as: It looks like . . . , This looks
like . . . , etc. There may be other facts which are relevant as
these are. But I have noticed that when I, at any rate, meet the
expression sense-data, these are the sorts of fact which come to
my mind.

I want, before I go on, to notice how narrowly Professor
Moore has conceived the problem of sense-data. It is common
among those who say that there are sense-data to say that
sounds, odors, tastes, etc., are sense-data; but it appears, apart
from the tell-no-tale phrase "in a certain respect," that Professor
Moore means by a sense-datum only that sort of thing which may
be taken to be the surface of something or other. In other words,
Professor Moore confines his use of the phrase sense-datum
only to what others would describe as *visual* sense-data. I find

Professor Moore's definition unusual in this respect, or mis-leading. If he does define "sense-data" in such a way as to include only "visual sense-data" then he defines the term in a way inconsistent with his own use of the term, for in a previous sentence he says, referring to sense-data: "I am at present seeing a great number of them and feeling others." At any rate his exposition excludes smells, tastes, and sounds. However that may be, the problem here is: What reflections would lead one to distinguish something which one would then say can or cannot be identical with the surface of one's hand which one is seeing?

The fact with respect to sounds, smells, and tastes is that they function in perceptual experiences in two ways. I can illustrate this best by a few pairs of sentences. Notice these:

> I hear a gnawing sound.
> I hear a rat.

> I smell an odor.
> I smell a rat.

> I taste a sour taste.
> I taste lemon.

The first of each of these pairs functions independently of the second, and one can describe sounds, odors, and tastes, without committing oneself to any sentence of the sort which is second in each pair. But the second does not function independently of the first. If you say: I hear a rat, then the question: What was the sound like?, is pertinent. In each case one may ask: What was the sound, or the odor, or the taste like? We are all acquainted with the descriptions of sounds, odors, and tastes. I need not, I think, enlarge upon this. If now someone held that there were sense-data and he meant by this that there were sounds, odors, and tastes, and that these are descriptively independent of rats and lemons, etc., there would, I think, be no controversy about this. There is no such question as: Is the sound or the odor of the rat identical with the surface of a rat, or the taste of a lemon identical with the surface of a lemon, or of that part of the lemon which I am tasting?

But now there are also certain similarities among facts of this following sort:

I hear a rat.
I smell a rat.
I taste a lemon.
I see a cloud.
I touch velvet.

And here, I take it, one is likely by reflection upon these sets of similarities to suppose that there must be some fact which corresponds to: I see a cloud, as: I hear a sound corresponds to: I hear a rat. And so too with: I touch velvet. Since, in other words, to hearing there corresponds a hearing sense-datum, and to smelling a smelling sense-datum, etc., so to seeing and to touching there must correspond seeing and touching sense-data. Actually, of course, there need not be such; and one part of the suggested parallel between hearing, smelling, and tasting, on the one hand, and seeing and touching, on the other, is missing. There are no descriptions of "sights" and "touches" which are independent conceptually of the descriptive characteristics of rats, lemons, clouds, velvet, etc. If you attempt to describe what you see, the same words which you use to describe the lemon or the cloud, will also serve to describe the purported sense-datum. So, if there is a sense-datum in these last cases, a new vocabulary will have to be engaged to perform the service. And so we get two different meanings for "is red" in the sentences "This (sense-datum) is red," and "This rose is red." This sort of accommodation is the consequence of the assumption that just as there are auditory sense-data so there must be visual sense-data. We make up for the deficiency in the facts from which we start by inventing a new vocabulary. Unfortunately we are compelled to use the same words which have otherwise per-formed an unambiguous service. It also follows that, if in the respect noted, seeing is like hearing, then as one is able, in hearing a bird, to distinguish the sound of the bird, so in seeing a hand one is able to pick out a corresponding visual sense-datum. The effect of these analogies may be so strong as to lead one to say that there must be a sense-datum.

These analogies do not however provide the only motive. Consider mirror reflections. Mirror reflections are like sounds and odors and tastes in a certain respect, and they are like lemons and clouds and velvet in another respect. The image of a lemon or a cloud is like a sound or an odor, in that the image is descriptively independent of the description of any lemon or cloud. On the other hand, the description of an image of a lemon or cloud is unlike the description of a sound or odor, in that the descriptive items which compose it are engaged also in describing lemons and clouds. Now how do these facts about images incline one to the belief that when one is looking at one's hand one is seeing a sense-datum, as one hears a sound? Perhaps in this way: If one is already impressed with the analogy between hearing and seeing, then one is inclined to believe that there is something which one is seeing which is distinguishable as the sound is from the bird one hears. Now if you look at your hand and try to discover this corresponding element, you may find your effort encouraged by the fact that there are things which are descriptively identical with what you are seeing which are nevertheless not the surfaces of lemons and clouds at all. That is, here you have in reflections what, since they are described in the same way in which lemons and clouds and hands are described, may very well be taken to be "the surfaces of lemons and clouds." So when you look at your hand, you may describe what you see just as you would describe the reflection of it in the mirror. Since then what you see is taken to be the surface of your hand, you at once understand how something might be described in this same way, and yet not be the surface of your hand at all. For the image in the mirror is not the surface of your hand. It is clear certainly that with this in mind you can, if you look at your hand, pick out something which is like what you saw in the mirror, when you raised your hand to the mirror.

There is one further set of facts which disposes us in the same way. Notice such sentences as these:

This sounds like a horse.

This smells like an onion.

This tastes like a peppermint.

This looks like a million dollars.

This feels like a sponge.

The use of these expressions is parallel to the first set described above. The first three are admittedly statements about a sound, a smell, and a taste. Now how about the fourth and the fifth? Well, they must also be about a "look" and about a "feel," the corresponding sense-data of seeing and touching, respectively. This does not now seem to me at all persuasive, and of course, for the same reason which I gave in discussing sounds, smells, etc. If one wished, for instance, to identify by description or by some other form of direction, the sound or smell in question, as distinguished from the horse or the onion, this is a simple matter. But if you wish to call attention to the "look" or to the "feel" in question there is no resort to doing this, save pointing out or identifying the "million dollars" or "the sponge" or whatever the object may be. In other words, what is called the "look" or the "feel" is not identifiable in the way in which the sound, or smell are identifiable. The use of the word "this" is commonly defined so as to apply to such uses as are involved in these first three sentences. But it is only by analogy that one comes to suppose that in the last two sentences the use is like that in the first three. Of course such a sentence as: "This looks like a million dollars," may apply also to a mirror-image, and we have already noticed what this means. The image of a girl who looks like a million dollars would also look like a million dollars. This means simply that they are described in the same way. Certainly from such facts as these, which we all admit, it does not follow that when you look at your hand, you can pick out something which is not your hand, of which you now say that it looks like your hand.

These are some of the facts upon which I reflect a little, when

I am led to the view that what Professor Moore has tried to persuade us is true. I want now to show that, if one does follow the lead of these facts, one is likely to use precisely the sort of language about "sense-data" which Professor Moore does use. If the analogy between seeing and hearing holds, then it follows in the first place that if you look at your right hand you will be able to pick out something, something which on the assumption given, corresponds to the sound in hearing. But this is a strange sort of direction, for, if I look at my right hand, nothing at all corresponds to the sound in case of hearing. There is simply my hand, or more conveniently as you will see in a moment, the surface of my hand. So I pick that out. Now I reflect, and describe what I see, reminded that what I see is like reflections in mirrors. I know, of course, that mirror-reflections are not identical with the surfaces of any hands, no matter how perfect the image may be. Now, since this is like an image in all these respects, it can't be the surface of my hand at all, and this in spite of the fact that I thought at the outset that I was picking out the surface of my hand. If the only thing I could pick out was what I took to be the surface of my hand, and that is the sense-datum, and this is like the image in the mirror, then see what follows. The reflection in the mirror has no depth. I cannot prick it with a pin. Now then does the surface of my hand have depth? If you say that what you picked out is like the reflection in the mirror, and it has no depth, then if it is identical with the surface of my hand, then the surface of my hand also has no depth. Can that be? On the other hand, if you say that what I picked out is identical with the surface of my hand, and the surface of my hand has depth, are we then to allow that the sense-datum, like a hand's surface, has depth? Can I prick a sense-datum with a pin? This is the puzzle which I noticed previously when I discussed Professor Moore's use of the phrase "surface of my hand," and it arises from conceiving of the sense-datum as like a mirror-reflection, and at the same time as something which one can pick out. If when, on this basis, I look at my hand, and try to pick out a sense-datum, I must be

surprised to discover something which, though it may be in
certain respects like the image in the mirror, is also remarkably
unlike it. For, in spite of what all these facts already noticed
lead me to expect, I discover nothing but my hand.

I should like to labour this last point. Imagine the sort of
situation you would be in, if, upon the basis of such facts as I
have noticed, you were disposed to expect a sense-datum. What
would you say in trying to describe what you expect? First of
all, you might tell someone to look at his hand, on the expectation that just as if he heard a bird, there would be a sound to
identify, so here there would be something corresponding to the
sound. It also follows from the character of what you see, that
if there is something corresponding to the sound, that you could
pick it out. If this were all, one would be inclined to describe
what you might pick out as "a yellow patch," "a red patch," "a
canoid patch of brown," etc., and it is easy to see what in a case of
this sort has happened. People who invent expressions of this
sort are trying to find some expressions which parallel the
descriptions of sounds, but the parallel is deceptive. For, if in
looking at your hand you now try to pick out "a hand-shape of
pink," you will find yourself picking out the surface of your
hand, whereas in the case of a sound the relations between the
sound and the bird are obviously different. The description of
the sound is not a description of the bird. But there is no
necessity for pursuing this. It is only necessary that what you
pick out should, like the sound, be distinguishable from your
hand, or the surface of your hand. As it is, you know that
reflections in mirrors and images otherwise are distinguishable
from what they reflect and image, though they are not descriptively distinguishable from what they reflect and image. So we
formulate a description accordingly: Pick out what has the
characteristics of a mirror-reflection. Looking into the mirror,
holding your hand to the mirror, I might ask: What do you
see?, and what you would then give me as a description would
equally apply to your hand. Now then you look at your hand,
and describe your hand, for what will satisfy my request is just

that. Further, if you have already committed yourself to saying that there is something here which corresponds to the sound in the case of hearing the bird, then you will feel pretty sure that you have picked that out. But you will nevertheless be puzzled. For if you have picked out the sense-datum, then if someone says: Now pick out the surface of your hand, you will be unable to do so unless the sense-datum and the surface of your hand are identical. And if you then ask: Did I pick out the surface of my hand?, already assured that you did pick out the sense-datum, you will be inclined to say: That may be, for a sense-datum can be the surface of a hand. And you will be inclined to say this because, as I said before, the reflection and the surface of my hand are similar. But you will also be inclined to say that a sense-datum cannot be the surface.

III

I have tried, in the preceding sections, first of all to explore certain difficulties in the directions which Professor Moore gives for discovering what it is he means by a sense-datum, and second to try to discover what motives there are which lead us to expect that there are sense-data, and which lead us also to such curious descriptions of them. My thesis has been this: The obvious distinction between sounds, tastes, and smells in hearing, tasting, and smelling leads us to expect a corresponding something or other in the case of seeing and touching. So when I look at my hand, I am led to expect that there is a sense-datum in this case. So I may say that I can pick it out. But when I try to pick it out I am at a loss. There is only my hand. Now if I still persist in holding that there is a sense-datum present, I am bound to describe it in a peculiar way. I am likely to describe it in analogy with an image or mirror-reflection. I may go on to think of the sense-datum which must be there, as spread exceedingly thin over the surface of my hand, a kind of epidermis, and at the same time as looking just like my hand when the sense-datum has been removed. Now if I keep this

fixed in my mind, and look at my hand, and if I am asked: What
do you see?, I am supposed not to know what to say. Do I see
just an image spread over the surface of my hand like so much
surfacing surfaceless paint, or do I see the surface of my hand?
I think I can tell an image from the surface of my hand, but
I confess that I should be much distressed in the attempt to
distinguish the image of the surface of my hand laid neatly on
the surface of my hand and defined in such a way as to be
indistinguishable from the surface of my hand, from the surface
of my hand. But fortunately, as I think, at least, I am not led to
expect anything like images spread over the surface of my hand,
and if I did, I should try pricking the epidermis. As I have
noticed before, that the attempt to describe what "must" be
present is desperate is also apparent in the consequent use of
the expression "the surface of his hand." For we do not as a
matter of fact have any difficulty in identifying the surface of our
hands. If then there is some difficulty, that difficulty has not
been properly described. And the point of my essay is that the
supposed entity which is defined in terms of a confusion,
which is generated by sentential likenesses, misleads us and
catches us in linguistic pockets.

Rubber gloves, the image of my hand, another man's hand,
all of these I know how to distinguish from my hand, when I
look at my hand, and when I am in doubt. But I am not moved
by the suggestion that whenever I look at my hand an image of
my hand may be interposed between my hand and my eye. In
that case we should need to invent the theory of the Pre-
Established Harmony between the hand and the sense-datum.
But why suggest it?

Having come to the end of my essay I am now full of misgivings. I know that I have not refuted Professor Moore's view.
I have tried, however, teasing the words of Professor Moore's
exposition, to get the matter straight. And this is what has come
of it. May my betters rob me of my "darling follies," among
which betters I have long counted first Professor Moore.

THE EXPRESSION THEORY OF ART

THE EXPRESSION THEORY OF ART is, I suppose, the most commonly held of all theories of art. Yet no statement of it seems to satisfy many of those who expound it. And some of us find all statements of it baffling. I propose in what follows to examine it carefully. In order to do this, I want first of all to state the question which gives rise to the theory and then to follow the lead of that question in providing an answer. I am eager to do this without using the language of the expression theory. I intend then to examine the language of that theory in order to discover whether it may reasonably be interpreted to mean what is stated in my answer. In this way I expect to indicate an important ambiguity in the use of the word "expression," but more emphatically to expose confusions in the use of the word "emotion." This then may explain the bafflement.

I

And now I should like to describe the sort of situation out of which by devious turnings the phrase "expression of emotion" may be conceived to arise.

Imagine then two friends who attend a concert together. They go together untroubled. On the way they talk about two girls,

Reprinted from "Philosophical Analysis: A Collection of Essays," edited by Max Black, © *1950, by permission of Prentice-Hall, Inc., Englewood Cliffs, New Jersey.*

about communism and pie on earth, and about a silly joke they once laughed at and now confess to each other that they never understood. They were indeed untroubled and so they entered the hall. The music begins, the piece ends, the applause intervenes, and the music beings again. Then comes the intermission and time for small talk. Octave, a naive fellow, who loves music, spoke first. "It was lovely, wasn't it? Very sad music, though." Verbo, for that was the other's name, replied: "Yes, it was very sad." But the moment he said this he became uncomfortable. He fidgeted in his seat, looked askance at his friend, but said no more aloud. He blinked, he knitted his brows, and he muttered to himself. "Sad music, indeed! Sad? Sad music?" Then he looked gloomy and shook his head. Just before the conductor returned, he was muttering to himself, "Sad music, crybaby, weeping willows, tear urns, sad grandma, sad, your grandmother!" He was quite upset and horribly confused. Fortunately, about this time the conductor returned and the music began. Verbo was upset but he was a good listener, and he was soon reconciled. Several times he perked up with "There it is again," but music calms, and he listened to the end. The two friends walked home together but their conversation was slow now and troubled. Verbo found no delight in two girls, in pie on earth, or in old jokes. There was a sliver in his happiness. At the corner as he parted with Octave, he looked into the sky, "Twinkling stars, my eye! Sad music, my ear!" and he smiled uncomfortably. He was miserable. And Octave went home, worried about his friend.

So Verbo went home and went to bed. To sleep? No, he couldn't sleep. After four turns on his pillow, he got up, put a record on the phonograph, and hoped. It didn't help. The sentence "Sad, isn't it?" like an imp, sat smiling in the loudspeaker. He shut off the phonograph and paced the floor. He fell asleep, finally, scribbling away at his table, like any other philosopher.

This then is how I should like to consider the use of the phrase "expression of emotion." It may be thought of as arising out of such situations as that I have just described. The use of emotional terms—sad, gay, joyous, calm, restless, hopeful, playful, etc.—in describing music, poems, pictures, etc., is indeed common. So long as such descriptions are accepted and understood in innocence, there will be, of course, no puzzle. But nearly everyone can understand the motives of Verbo's question "How can music be sad?" and of his impulsive "It can't, of course."

Let us now consider two ways in which one may safely escape the expression theory.

Imagine Verbo at his desk, writing. This is what he now writes and this gives him temporary relief. "Every time I hear that music I hear that it's sad. Yet I persist in denying it. I say that it cannot be sad. And now what if I were wrong? If every day I met a frog, and the frog said to me that he was a prince, and that there were crown jewels in his head ('wears yet a precious jewel in his head'), no doubt I should begin by calling him a liar. But the more I'd consider this the more troubled I should be. If I could only believe him, and then treat him like a prince, I'd feel so much better. But perhaps *this* would be more like the case of this music: Suppose I met the frog and every day he said to me, 'I can talk,' and then went on talking and asked me, 'Can I talk?' then what would I do? And that's very much how it is with the music. I hear the music, and there it is again, sad, weeping. It's silly to deny this. See now, how it is? There's a little prince, the soul of a prince, in the frog, and so there's the soul in this music, a princess, perhaps. See then how rude I was denying this princess her weeping. Why shouldn't music have a soul too? Why this prejudice in favor of lungs and livers? And it occurs to me that this is precisely how people have talked about music and poems. Art lives, doesn't it? And how did Milton describe a good book? Didn't Shelley pour out his soul? And isn't there soul and spirit in the music? I remember now that the poet Yeats recommended some such thing. There are spirits; the air is full of them. They haunt music, cry in it. They dance in poems, and laugh. Pan-psychism for the habitation of all delicacies! So this is how it is, and there is neither joke nor puzzle in this sad music. There's a sad soul in it."

And then it was that Verbo fell asleep. His resistance to the music had melted away as soon as he gave up his curious prejudice in favor of animal bodies, as soon as he saw that chords and tones, like rhymes and rhythms, may sigh and shed invisible tears. Tears without tear glands—oh, I know the vulgar habit! But surely tones may weep. Consider now how reasonable all this is. Verbo is suddenly surprised to discover something which he has always known, namely that music is sad. And the discovery startles him. Why? Because in connection with this, he thinks of his sister Sandra (Cassie to all who saw her cry). And he knows what her being sad is like. She sobs, she wipes her eyes, and she tells her troubles. Cassie has a soul, of course. So Cassie is sad and the music is sad. So the question for Verbo is "How can the music be like Cassie?" and he gives the answer "Why shouldn't there be a soul of the music, that flits in and flits out (People die too!) and inhabits a sonata for a half-hour? Or why shouldn't there be a whole troupe of them? 'The music is sad' is just like 'Cassie is sad,' after all. And Octave who was not disturbed was quite right for he must have a kind of untroubled belief in spirits. He believes in the frog-prince, in the nymphs in the wood, and in the psyche of the sonnet."

This then is one way of going to sleep. But there is another one, and it is based upon much the same sort of method. Both accept as the standard meaning for "The music is sad," the meaning of "Cassie is sad." We saw how Verbo came to see that the meaning is the same, and how then it was true in the case of the music. He might however have decided that the meaning certainly was the same, but that as applied to the music it simply made no sense at all, or was plainly false. Souls in sonnets! Don't be silly. There is the story about Parmenides well-known to all readers of Dionoges,[1] which will illustrate the sort of thing I have in mind. According to the story, Parmenides and his finicky friend Zeno once went to a chariot race. The horses and chariots had been whizzing past and the race had

[1] An author of no repute at all, not to be confused with Diogenes.

been quite exciting. During the third round, at one turn a
chariot broke an axle and horse and chariot and rider went
through the fence. It was a marvelous exhibition of motion
done to a turn at a turn. Parmenides was enjoying himself
thoroughly. He clutched at the railing and shouted at the top of
his voice, "Go, Buceph! Run!" The race is close. But at about
the seventh round, with Buceph now some part of a parasang
behind, Parmenides began to consider: "Half the distance in
half the time; a quarter of the length of a horse in a quarter of
the pace it takes...." Suddenly, before the race was half over,
Parmenides turned to Zeno. "Zeno," he said, "this is impossible." Zeno, who was ready for his master, retorted, "I
quit looking a long time ago." So they left the chariot race, a
little embarrassed at their nonexistence showing as they walked,
but they did not once look back to see how Buceph was doing.

This then is the story about Parmenides. It may be, of course,
that this story is not true; it may be one of Dionoges' little jokes.
But our concern is not with Parmenides. The point is that it
illustrates a certain way of disposing of puzzles. Parmenides has
been disciplined to a certain use of such words as " run," "go,"
" turn," " walk," etc., so that when he is thoughtful and has all
his careful wits about him, he never uses those words. He is then
fully aware that all forms of motion are impossible. Nevertheless
the eyes are cunning tempters. In any case as soon as Parmenides
reflects, he buries himself in his tight-fitting vocabulary, and
shuts out chariots and horses, and Buceph, as well. "Motion is
impossible, so what am I doing here? Less than nothing. N'est
pas is not." This disposition of the puzzle is, of course, open
only to very strong men. Not many of those people who believe
in the impossibility of motion are capable of leaving a horse
race, especially when some fleet favorite is only a few heads
behind.

Now something like this was a possibility also for Verbo.
When, puzzled as he was, asking "How can that be?" he hit
upon the happy solution " Why not?" But he might surely have
said, stamping his foot, "It can't be." And in order then to

avoid the pain of what can't be, he might have sworn off music altogether. No more concerts, no more records! The more radical decision is in such cases most effective. One can imagine Parmenides, for instance, sitting out the race, with his eyes closed, and every minute blinking and squinting, hoping he'd see nothing. So too Verbo might have continued to listen to music, but before every hearing invigorating his resolution never to say that the music was sad. Success in this latter enterprise is not likely to be successful, and for anyone who has already been puzzled it is almost certainly futile.

We have not noticed two ways in which one may attempt to rid oneself of the puzzle concerning "The music is sad," but incidentally we have also noticed the puzzle. The puzzle is identified with the question "How can music be sad?" We have also noticed how easy it is, once having asked the question, to follow it with "Well, it can't." I want now to go on to consider the expression theory in the light of the question "How can it be?" In effect, the expression theory is intended to relieve people who are puzzled by music, etc. They listen and they say that the music is sad. They ask, troubled and shaking their heads, "How can it be?" Then along comes the expression theory. It calms them, saying, "Don't you see that the music expresses sadness and that this is what you mean by its being sad?" The puzzled one may be calmed too, if he isn't careful. In any case, I propose to consider the question "How can it be?" before going on further.

This question "How can it be?" is apparently then not a question primarily about the music. One listens to the music and hears all that there is to hear. And he is sure that it is sad. Nevertheless when he notices this and then returns to the music to identify just what is sad in it, he is baffled. If someone, for instance, had said that there is a certain succession of four notes on the flute, in this music, and he now sought to identify them, he could play the music, and when they came along, he would exclaim, "There they are," and that would be just what he aimed at. Or again if someone had said that a certain passage was very painful, and he explained that he meant by this that when it is heard one feels a stinging at one's finger tips, then again one could play the music and wait for the stinging. Neither is it like the question which leaped out of the surprise of the farmer at the birth of his first two-headed calf. He looked, amazed, and exclaimed, "Well, I'll be switched! How can that be?" He bedded the old cow, Janus, tucked in the calf, and went to consult his book. He did not stand muttering, looking at the calf, as Verbo did listening to the record on the phonograph. He took out his great book, *The Cow*, and read the chapter entitled "Two Heads Are Better than One?" He read statistics and something about the incidence of prenatal collusion and decided to keep an eye on collaborators among his herd. And that was all. When now it comes to "The music is sad," there's no such easy relief. What is there to listen for? What statistics are there?

We have noticed before how Verbo settled his difficulty. He did this, but not by examining the music any further. He simply knew that the music was sad, and supplied the invisible tears, the unheard sobs, the soul of the music. If you had asked him to identify the tears, the unheard sobs, the soul of the music, he could not have done this. He might have tried, of course, and then he would have been baffled too. But the point is that he tries to think of the sadness of the music in the way in which he thinks of Cassie's sadness. Now we may be ready to explain the predicament, the bafflement. It arises from our trying to understand our use of the sentence " The music is sad" in terms of our uses of other sentences very much like this. So Verbo understands in terms of the sentence "Cassie is sad." One can imagine him saying to himself, "I know what sadness is, of course, having Cassie in the house, so that must be how it is with the music." Happily, as in the case of Parmenides, he thought of only one use, and as with a sharp knife he cut the facts to suit the knife. But suppose now that there are several uses of sentences much like " The music is sad"; what then? Is it like this use or this use or this use? And suppose that

sometimes it's like this and at other times like this, and sometimes like both. Suppose further that one is only vaguely aware
that this is so, and that one's question "How can that be?" is
not stated in such a way as to make this possibility explicit,
would it then be any wonder that there is bafflement?

Let us admit then that the use of "The music is sad" is
baffling, and that without some exploration, the question "How
can that be?" cannot be dealt with. Merely listening to the
music will not suffice. We must then explore the uses of other
sentences which are or may be similar to this, and we may hope
that in this process we may see the expression theory emerge.
At any rate, we'll understand what we are about.

II

What now are some of these other types of sentences which
might be helpful? Well, here are a few that might serve:
"Cassie is sad," "Cassie's dog is sad," "Cassie's book is sad,"
"Cassie's face is sad." Perhaps, one or the other of these will do.

Though we have already noticed how Verbo came to use
"Cassie is sad," I should like to consider that sentence further.
Verbo understood this. When, as he remembered so well, the
telephone call came and little Cassie answered—she had been
waiting for that call—she was hurt. Her voice had broken as she
talked, and he knew that the news had been bad. But he did not
think she would take it so hard. And when she turned to him
and he asked her what the man had said, at first her chin
quivered and she didn't speak. Then she moved towards him and
fell into his arms, sobbing: "Poor Felicia, poor Felicia!" He
stroked her hair and finally when she was calm, she began to
pour out her confidences to him. She loved her cat so; they had
been brought up together, had had their milk from the same
bottle, and had kept no secrets from each other. And now the
veterinary had called to say that she had had another fit. And
she burst into tears again. This was some years ago. Cassie is
older now.

But this is not the only way in which "Cassie is sad" is used. Verbo had often heard his father and mother remark that it was good that Cassie could cry. They used to quote some grandmother who made a proverb in the family. It went: "Wet pillows are best." She had made this up many years ago when some cousin came to sudden grief. This cousin was just on the verge of planned happiness, when the terrible news came. (Her picture is the third in the album.) She received the news in silence and never spoke of it or referred to it as long as she washed the dishes in her father's house, for, as you may have guessed, she never married. She never cried either. No one ever heard her sniffling in the middle of the night. She expressed no regrets. And she never told cat or mirror anything. Once she asked for a handkerchief, but she said she had a cold. All the family knew what had happened, of course, and everyone was concerned, but there was nothing to do. And so she was in many ways changed. She was drooping, she had no future, and she tried to forget her past. She was not interested. They all referred to her as their sad cousin, and they hoped that she would melt. But she didn't. Yet how can Cassie's cousin be sad if she never cries?

Well, there is a third use of "Cassie is sad." Tonight Cassie, who is eighteen now, quite a young lady, as the neighbors say, goes up to her room with her cat, her big book, and a great bowl of popcorn. She settles into her chair, tells kitty to get down, munches buttery corn, and reads her book. Before very long she is quite absorbed in what she reads and feels pretty bad. Her eyes fill with tears and the words on the page swim in the pool. It's so warm and so sweet and so sad! She would like to read this aloud, it's so wonderful, but she knows how the sadness in her throat would break her words in two. She's so sorry; she's so sad. She raises her eyes, closes them, and revels in a deep-drawn sigh. She takes up a full hand of popcorn and returns to her sadness. She reads on and eats no more corn. If she should sob in corn, she might choke. She does sob once, and quite loud, so that she is startled by it. She doesn't want to be heard sobbing over her book. Five minutes later she lays her book aside, and in a playful mood, twits her cat, pretending she's a little bird. Then, walking like old Mother Hubbard, she goes to the cupboard to get her poor cat a milk.

Cassie is sad, isn't she? Is she? Now that you consider it, she isn't really sad, is she? That cozy chair, that deliberate popcorn, that playing sparrow with her cat, that old Mother Hubbard walk—these are not the manners of a sad girl. She hasn't lost her appetite. Still one can see at once how we come to describe her in this way. Those are not phony tears, and she's as helpless in her sobs and in keeping her voice steady and clear as she was years ago when her dear cat had that fit. And she can, if you are so curious, show you in the book just what made her feel so sad. So you see it is very much like the case in which Cassie was sad. There's an obvious difference, and a similarity too. And now if you balk at this and don't want to say that Cassie in this situation is sad, your objection is intelligible. On the other hand if Cassie herself laughingly protests, "Oh, yes, I was sad," that will be intelligible too. This then may serve as an illustration of the way in which a puzzle which might become quite serious is fairly easily dealt with. How can Cassie be sad, eating popcorn and playing she's a sparrow?

In order to make this clear, consider Cassie now a grown woman, and an accomplished actress. She now reads that same passage which years ago left her limp as a willow, but her voice is steady and clear, and there are no tears. She understands what she reads and everyone says that she reads it with such feeling—it's so sad!—but there isn't a sign of emotion except for the reading itself, which as I said, goes along smoothly and controlled even to each breath and syllable. So there are no wet eyes, no drunken voice, and not a sob that isn't in the script. So there. Is she sad? I take it not. The spoken words are not enough. Tears, real tears, a voice that breaks against a word, sighs that happen to one, suffered sobs—when the reading occasions these, then you might say that Cassie was sad. Shall we say however, that the reading is sad? How can that be? Well, you see, don't you?

Let us now attend to a sentence of a different type: "Cassie's dog is sad." Can a dog be sad? Can a dog hope? Can a dog be disappointed? We know, of course, how a Cartesian would answer. He might very well reply with this question, "Can a locomotive be sad?" Generous, he might allow that a locomotive might look sad, and so give you the benefit of a sad look for your dog. But can a dog be sad? Well, our dog can. Once during the summer when Cassie left her for three weeks, you should have seen her. She wouldn't look at the meatiest bone. She'd hang her head and look up at you as woebegone as a cow. And she'd walk as though her four hearts would break. She didn't cry, of course, and there were no confidences except those touching ones that come by way of petting and snuggling and looking into those wailing eyes. In any case our dog acted very much like that sad cousin who couldn't cry. She had plenty of reason, much too much, but she kept her wellings-up down. It's clear in any case what I mean when I say that our dog was sad. You mustn't expect everything from a sad dog.

So we pass to another type of sentence: "Cassie's book is sad." Well, obviously books don't cry. Books do not remember happier days nor look upon hopes snuffed out. Still, books that are sad, must have something to do with sadness, so there must be sadness. We know, of course. Books make people sad. Cassie reads her book and in a few minutes if she's doing well, she's sad. Not really sad, of course, but there are real tears, and one big sob that almost shook the house. It certainly would be misleading to say that it was imaginary sadness, for the sadness of Cassie isn't imagined by anyone, not even by herself. What she reads on the other hand is imaginary. What she reads about never happened. In this respect it's quite different from the case in which she is overwhelmed by the sad news over the telephone. That was not imaginary, and with the tears and sobs there was worry, there was distress. She didn't go twittering about, pretending she was a little bird five minutes after that happened. So a sad book is a book that makes Cassie, for instance, sad. You ask, "Well, what are you crying about?" And she says, "Booh, you just read this." It's true that that is how you will find out, but you may certainly anticipate too that it will be a story about a little boy who died, a brave little boy who had stood up bravely for his father, about a new love and reconciliation come almost too late, about a parting of friends and tender feelings that will die, and so on. At any rate, if this is what it is like, you won't be surprised. It's a sad book.

There is one further sentence to consider: "Cassie's face is sad." The same sort of thing might be said about her speaking, about her walk, about her eyes, etc. There is once again an obvious way of dealing with this. What makes you say her face is sad? Anyone can tell. See those tear stains and those swollen eyes. And those curved lines, they all turn down. Her face is like all those sad faces in simple drawings where with six strokes of my neighbor's pencil I give you "Sad-Eye, the Sorry Man." The sad face is easily marked by these few unmistakable signs. Pull a sad face, or droop one, and then study it. What have you done? In any case, I am supposing that there is another use of "Cassie's face is sad," where this simplicity is absent. Oh, yes, there may be certain lines, but if you now ask, "And is this all you mean by Cassie's face being sad," the answer may very well be "No." Where then is the sadness? Take a long look and tell me. Cassie, hold still. The sadness is written all over her face, and I can't tell you it's here and not there. The more I look, the more I see it. The sadness in this case is not identified with some gross and simple signs. And you are not likely to find it there in some quick glance. Gaze into that face, leisurely, quietly, gently. It's as though it were composed not of what is sad in all sad faces, but rather of what is sad only in each sad face you've ever known. This sad face is sad but when you try now to tell someone what is sad in it, as you might with the drawing I made, you will have nothing to say. But you may say, "Look, and you will see." It is clear, of course, that when Cassie's face is sad, she need not be sad at all. And certainly when you look as you do, you need not be sad.

We have noticed briefly several types of sentences similar to

"The music is sad," and we have seen how in respect to several of these the same sort of puzzling might arise that arose in respect to "The music is sad." We have also seen how in respect to these more obvious cases this puzzling is relieved. The puzzling is relieved by discerning the similarity between the offending use and some other use or uses. And now I should like to ask whether the puzzle concerning "The music is sad" might not also be relieved in some similar fashion. Is there not a use of some type of sentence, familiar and relatively untroubled, which is like the use of " The music is sad"?

We have these types of sentences now ready at our disposal: There are two uses of "Cassie is sad," in the first of which she is concerned about her cat, and in the second of which she is cozy and tearful, reading her book. We have "Cassie's cousin is sad," in which Cassie's cousin has real cause but no tears, and "Cassie's dog is sad," in which her dog is tearless as her cousin, but with a difference of course. You could scarcely say that Fido restrained his tears. Then there were the uses of "Cassie's face is sad" and "Cassie's reading is sad." And, of course, there is the use of "Cassie's book is sad." I am going to take for granted that these uses are also intelligible. Now then is the use of "The music is sad" similar to any of these?

I suppose that if the question is stated in this way, one might go on by pointing out a similarity between it and each one of these other types of sentences. But what we must discover is enough similarity, enough to relieve the puzzle. So the question is: To which use is the use of "The music is sad" most similar? Certainly not to "Cassie is sad (about her cat)," nor to "Cassie's cousin is sad," nor to "Cassie's dog is sad."

There are two analogies that one may hopefully seize upon. The first is this: "Cassie is sad, reading a book," is very much like "Verbo is sad, listening to music." And this first is also very much like "Cassie is sad, hearing the news over the telephone." And just as the first involves "The book is sad," so the second involves "The music is sad," and the third involves " The news is sad." Now let us consider the first. Reading the book is one

thing, and feeling sad is quite another, and when you say that
the book is sad, you mean by this something like this: When
Cassie reads, she feels sad about what she reads. Her feeling sad
refers to her tears, her sobs, etc. So too listening to the music
and hearing it is one thing, and feeling sad is another, and when
you say that the music is sad, you mean that while Verbo listens
to the music, he feels sad. And shall we add that he feels sad
about it? This might, if you like, refer to something like his
half-tears, sub-sobs, etc.

Suppose now we try to relieve Verbo in this way. We say,
"Don't you see? 'This music is sad' is like 'The book is sad.'
You understand that. That's very much like 'The news is sad.'"
Will that satisfy him? I think that if he is very sharp, it won't.
He may say, "I can see how 'The book is sad' is like 'The news
is sad.' But when it comes to these you can easily point out the
disturbance, the weeping, but the music—that's different. Still
there might be something." What now bothers him?

I think what bothers him may be explained in this way. When
you say that a book is sad, or a certain passage in a book is sad,
you may mean one or other or both of two things. You may
mean what has already been defined by the analogy above. But
you may also mean something else. The following illustration
may exhibit this. Imagine Cassie, then, in her big chair, reading,
and this is the passage she reads:

"I say this in case we become bad," Alyosha went on, " but
there's no reason why we should become bad, is there, boys?
Let us be, first and above all, kind, then honest, and let
us never forget each other! I say that again. I give you my
word, for my part, that I'll never forget one of you. Every
face looking at me now I shall remember even for thirty
years. Just now Kolya said to Kartashov that he did not
care to know whether he exists or not. But I cannot forget
that Kartashov exists and that he is blushing now as he did
when he discovered the founders of Troy, but is looking at
me with his jolly, kind, dear little eyes. Boys, my dear boys,
let us all be generous and brave like Ilusha, clever, brave

and generous like Kolya (though he will be ever so much cleverer when he grows up), and let us all be as modest, as clever and sweet as Kartashov. But why am I talking about those two! You are all dear to me, boys, from this day forth I have a place in my heart for you all, and I beg you to keep a place in your hearts for me! Well, and who has united us in this kind, good feeling which we shall remember, and intend to remember all our lives? Who, if not Ilusha, the good boy, the dear boy, precious to us forever! Let us never forget him. May his memory live forever in our hearts from this time forth."

Cassie reads this and Cassie cries. Let us call this Cassie's sadness. But is there now any other emotion, any other sadness, present? Well, there may very well be. There may be the Alyosha emotion. Whether that is present however depends upon how the passage in question is read. It may be read in such a way, that though Cassie understands all she reads, and so knows about the Alyosha emotion, yet she will miss it. This will be the case if she cries through the reading of it. If she reads the passage well, controlled, clear, unfalteringly, with feeling, as we say, which does not mean with crying, then the Alyosha emotion will be present. Otherwise only signs of it will be present. Anyone who has tried to read such a passage well, and who has sometimes failed and sometimes succeeded, will understand what I have in mind. Now then we have distinguished the Cassie emotion and the Alyosha emotion. They may be present together, but only, I think, when the Cassie emotion is relatively weak. And so when someone says that the passage in question is sad, then in order to understand we must ask, "Is it sad in the Cassie emotion or is it sad in the Alyosha emotion?"

And now we are prepared again to examine the analogy: "The music is sad" is like "The book is sad," where it is sad with the Alyosha emotion. This now eliminates the messiness of tears. What we mean by Alyosha's emotion involves no tears, just as the sadness of the music involves no tears. And this now may remind us of Cassie reading the passage, cool, collected, reading with feeling. But more to the point it suggests the sentence "Cassie's face is sad." For see, when the music is sad, there are no tears, and when the passage is read, well read, there are no tears. And so when I look into this face and find it sad, there are no tears. The sadness in all these cases may be unmistakable, and yet in none of these is there anything to which I might now draw your attention, and say, "That's how I recognize it as sad." Even in the case of the reading, it isn't the sentences, it isn't the subject, that makes it sad. The sadness is in the reading. Like a musical score, it too may be played without feeling. And it isn't now as though you both read and have these feelings. There is nothing but the reading, and the feeling is nothing apart from this. Read the passage with and without feeling, and see that the difference consists in a difference in the reading. What baffles in these cases is that when you use the word "sadness" and the phrase "with feeling," you are certain to anticipate sadness and feeling in the ordinary sense. But if the sadness is in the sounds you make, reading or playing, and in the face, once you are forewarned you need no longer anticipate anything else. There is sadness which is heard and sadness which is seen.

This then is my result. "The music is sad" is like "The book is sad," where "The book is sad" is like "The face is sad." But "The music is sad" is sometimes also like "The book is sad," where "The book is sad" is like "The news is sad." If exhibiting these analogies is to be helpful, then, of course, this depends on the intelligibility of such sentences as "The book is sad," "The face is sad," "The news is sad," etc.

III

So far I have tried to do two things. I have tried to state the problem to which the expression theory is addressed, and then I have gone on to work at the solution of that problem in the way in which this statement of the problem itself suggests that it be worked out. In doing this I have sought deliberately to avoid the language of the expression theory.

Here then is the phrase to be studied. The expression theory maintains: The music is sad means: The music is the expression of sadness or of a certain sadness. The crucial word is the word "expression." There are now at least two contexts which determine the use of that word, one is the language of emotion, and the other is the language of or about language.

Let us consider first the use of the word "expression" in the language of emotion. In the discussion of the types of sentences above, it will be remembered that Cassie's cousin is sad, but doesn't cry. She does not "express" her emotion. Cassie on the other hand carries on, crying, sobbing, and confiding in everyone. She "expresses" her emotion, and the expression of her emotion is tears, noises, talk. That talk is all about her cat, remember. When she reads her book, she carries on in much the same way. In this latter case, there was some question as to whether there was really any emotion. She was so sad, remember, and ate popcorn. But in terms of what we just now said, whether there is emotion or not, there certainly is "expression" of emotion. These tears are just as wet as other tears, and her sobs are just as wet too. So in both cases there is expression of emotion, and in the first case there is emotion, thick as you please, but in the second case, it's not that thick. It appears then that you might find it quite natural to say that there is expression of emotion but no emotion, much as you might say that there was the thought of an elephant, but no elephant. This may not seem so strange, however, if we reflect that as in the case of Cassie's cousin, there may be emotion, but no or very little expression of emotion.

In order to probe the further roots of the uses of this phrase, it may be useful to notice that the language of emotion is dominantly the language of water. So many of our associations with the word "emotion" are liquid. See then: Emotions well up. Children and young girls bubble over. There are springs of emotion. A sad person is a deep well. Emotions come in waves; they are like the tides; they ebb and flow. There are floods and "seas of passion." Some people gush; some are turbulent.

Anger boils. A man blows up like a boiler. Sorrow overwhelms. The dear girl froze. We all know the theory of humors. In any case, it is easy enough, in this way, to think of a human being as like a reservoir and an everflowing pool and stream of emotions. All flow on toward a dam, which may be raised or lowered, and over and through which there is a constant trickle. Behind the dam are many currents, hot, cold, lukewarm, swift, slow, steady, rippling, smooth. And there are many colors. Perhaps we should say that currents are never exhausted and do not altogether trickle away. Emotions, like our thoughts, are founded, ready to be tapped, to be rippled, to be disturbed.

Let us see how the term "expression" fits into this figure. How was it with Cassie's cousin? Well, once there was a clear, smooth-flowing current of affection, and it flowed, trickle, trickle, over the dam in happy anticipation and a chestful of hope's kitchen and linen showers. And suddenly a planet falls, in the form of a letter, into that deep and flowing pool. Commotion follows, waves leap, eddies swirl. The current rushes on to the dam. And what happens? The dam rises. Cassie's cousin resists, bites her lip, intensifies her fist. She keeps the current back. Her grief is impounded. She does not "express" her emotion. And what happens to Cassie, when she felt so bad about the cat? That's easy. Then too there was a disturbance. The current came down, splashed over the dam which did not rise at all, and it flowed away in a hurly-burly of "Oh! It's awful! My poor kitty!" Cassie let herself go. She "expressed" her emotion.

The use of the word "expression" in the light of this figure is, I take it, clear enough. And the use of the word in this way describes a familiar difference in the way in which good news and bad news may affect us. And now we may ask, "And is it something like this that people have in mind when they say that art is the expression of emotion?" Certainly something like this, at least part of the time. Consider how Wordsworth wrote about poetry: "Poetry is the spontaneous overflow of powerful emotions." Overflow! This suggests the pool and the dam and the "powerful" current. An emotion, lying quiet, suddenly gets going and goes over. There is spontaneity, of course. No planet falls and no cat is sick. The emotion is unprovoked. There is also the common view that artists are people who are more emotional than other people. They are temperamental. This once again suggests the idea that they have particular need of some overflow. Poetry is a little like blowing off steam. Write poetry or explode!

This isn't all that Wordsworth said about poetry. In the same context he said: "Poetry is emotion recollected in tranquility." Again this suggests a hiding place of emotion, a place where past heartaches are stored, and may be taken up again, "recollected." We store ideas. We also put away emotions. So we have the pool as we had the pool before in describing Cassie's cousin and Cassie. But now we have something else, "the spontaneous over-flow" and the "recollection in tranquility."

Let us consider this for a moment, again in order to notice the use of the word "expression." Cassie hears bad news and cries. She "expresses" her emotion. The emotion is aroused and out it flows. What now happens in the case of the poet? Ostensibly in his case too emotions are aroused, but they do not flow out. Poets do not cry enough. Emotions are stored up, blocked. Emotions accumulate. And what happens now? Well, one of two things may happen. Emotions may quite suddenly leap up like spray, and find a way out, or again a poet may dip into the pool with his word dipper, and then dip them out. It's as though the emotions come over the dam in little boats (the poems) and the little boats may be used over and over again to carry over new surges. And this too may be described in this way: The poet "expresses" his emotion. Cassie cries. The real incident is sufficient. The poet does not cry. The real incident is not suffi-cient. He's got to make poems in order to cry. All men must cry. This may seem a bit fantastic, but this sort of phantasy is common in explaining something as old, for instance, as Aristotle's use of the word "catharsis."

The analogy which we have tried to exhibit now is this one: As Cassie "expresses" her emotion at hearing the news, so the poet or reader "expresses" his emotion at reading the poem. The news and the poem arouse or evoke the respective emotions. Now most people who expound the expression theory are not content with this analogy. They say that Cassie merely vents or discharges her emotion. This is not "expression" of emotion. Cassie merely gets rid of her emotion. And what does the poem do? Perhaps in terms of our figure we may say: It ripples it, blows a gentle wind over it, like a bird skimming the water. At any rate the emotion stays. And so the theory seeks a more suitable analogy and finds it conveniently in the language about language.

I should like first to notice certain distinctions which lead to this shift from the first to the second analogy. In the first place poems and music are quite different from the occasions that make Cassie and Cassie's cousin so sad. Tones on a piano and a faithless lover or a dying cat are not much alike, and this is enough to disturb the analogy. But there is also an unmistakable difference in the use of the word "emotion" in the two cases. An "emotion recollected in tranquility" is, after all, as I suggested before, more like a ripple than like a tempest. It is, accordingly, these distinctions that determine the shift. It may be useful to notice that the general form of the first analogy is retained in the second. For the poem and the music are still conceived as "arousing," as "evoking," the emotion.

The new analogy accordingly is this one: Music "expresses" sadness (art expresses emotion) as sentences "express" ideas. And now, I think, it is easy to see why this analogy should have been seized upon. In the first place so much of art involves symbols, sentences themselves, and representations. There are horses in pictures. It is quite easy then to fall into regarding art as symbolic, that is, as like sentences. And now just as sentences symbolize ideas and serve to evoke them as distinguished from real things, of which ideas are more like shadows, so too music and poems serve to evoke emotions of a peculiar sort, emotions which are like the shadows of real emotions. So this analogy is certainly an improvement. Art is after all an artifice, like sentences, and the emotions involved are related to the real things in much the way that ideas are to real things, faint copies. All this fits in very well with the idea that art is like a dream, a substitute of real life, a vicarious more of what you cannot have, a shadowland.

And now how does this analogy succeed?

Before answering this question, I should like to notice the use of the words "evoking" and "arousing." Sentences "evoke" ideas. As one spieler I know, says: "When I read a sentence, an idea pops into my head." Pops! This is something like what, according to the analogy, is meant by sentences "expressing" ideas. I am not interested in criticizing this at this point. I wish only to clarify ideas. Pop! Consider the sentence "The elephant ate a jumbo peanut." If at the moment when you read this sentence you see in your mind's eye a big elephant nuzzling around a huge peanut, this will illustrate what "evoking" is like. The sentence evokes; the idea pops. There is the sentence and there is this unmistakable seeing in your mind's eye. And if this happened, surely you would have got the idea. What I wish to point out is that it is this view or some similar view of how sentences work, that underlies this present analogy. They "evoke." But the word "evoke" has other contexts. It suggests spirits, witchcraft. The spirit of Samuel appearing at the behest of the witch of Endor is an "evocation." Spiritualistic mediums "evoke" the living spirits of the dead. And the point of this association is that the spirits are waiting, in the second or third canto of Dante's *Comedy*, perhaps, to be called. They are in storage like our ideas, like our emotions. And the word "arouse" is like the word "evoke." Whom do you arouse? The sleeper. And so, sleeping ideas and sleeping emotions lie bedded in that spacious dormitory—hush!—we call the mind. Waiting to be called! And why now have I made a point of this? Because this helps to fill out this analogy by which in particular we are led to use the word "feeling" or "emotion" in the language of the expression theory. The music "evokes," "arouses" feelings.

Now then, do poems and music and pictures evoke emotions as sentences evoke images? I think that they frequently do. Cassie reading her book may be cited as an instance. This seems to me a very common type of experience. It happens at the movies, in reading novels, and even in listening to music. People are moved to tears. If, accordingly, the expression theory were intended merely to describe experience of this sort, I should say, "Very well." In that case there would be no particular puzzle, beyond presenting this analogy clearly. But I, at least, am convinced that this is not all.

The difficulty then does not arise concerning experiences of this sort. The puzzle arises and remains most stubbornly where the sadness is dry-eyed. And here the analogy with language seems, at least, to be of no use. Cassie may read the passage with feeling, but without the flicker of an eyelash. And she may listen to sad music as cool and intent as she is gazing at a butterfly. She might say that it was more like watching, fascinated, the pain in a suffering face, herself quite undistressed. Santayana identifies the experience in this way: "Not until I confound the impressions (the music; the sentences) and suffuse the symbols with the emotions they arouse, and find joy and sweetness in the very words I hear, will the expressiveness constitute a beauty...."[2] I propose now to study this sentence.

Now notice how curious this is. Once more we have the sentences or the music. And these arouse emotions. This describes Cassie reading her book. So we might expect that Cassie would cry and would sob and so on. But this isn't all. Cassie is confused. Actually she is crying but she thinks the words are crying. She wipes her tears off those words. She sighs but the words heave. The sentence of Santayana suggests that she sees the sentences she reads through her tears and now her tears misserve her much as blue moods or dark glasses do. So Cassie looks through sadness and the sentence is tearful. What a pathetic fallacy! From confusion to suffusion! Are there mis-

[2] *Sense of Beauty* (New York: Charles Scribner's Sons, 1896), p. 149.

placed emotions? Imagine what this would be like where
sentences aroused not emotions but a toothache. And now you
confused the toothache with the sentence, and before someone
prevented you, you sent the sentence to the dentist.

Nevertheless, Santayana has almost certainly identified an
experience that is different from that in which Cassie is sad over
her book. We find "joy and sweetness in the very words " we
hear. Clearly, too, Santayana has been misled by these words
"joy and sweetness." For if there is joy and sweetness, where
should these be but where they usually are? Where is joy then
and where is sweetness? In the human breast, in the heart ("my
heart leaps up when I behold"), in the eye. And if you say this,
then indeed there must be some illusion. The sentence is like a
mirror that catches and holds what is in the heart. And so
artful are poets' sentences that the best readers are the best
confused. I want now, however, to suggest that indeed joy and
sweetness, and sadness too, are in the very words you hear. But
in that case, joy and sweetness must be of the sort that can be in
sentences. We must, accordingly, try to figure out what this
"joy and sweetness in the very words" is like. For even though,
making a mistake, one imagined they were in the words, their
being there must make some sense. And Santayana too does not
imagine that sentences cry.

Let me return now to the analogy: The music is sad is like:
The sentence expresses an idea. We saw before how the sentence
"The elephant ate a jumbo peanut" might be accompanied by
an image and how this was like sentences or music arousing
emotions. We want now to see how we might use the phrase
"joy and sweetness in the very words." Do we have a meaning
for "The idea in the very words you hear." Where is the idea of
the elephant eating a jumbo peanut? Suppose we say, "It's in
the very words you hear." Have you ever seen, in your mind's
eye, that is, an elephant eating a peanut in the very words you
hear? A sentence is like a circus tent? I do not suppose that
anyone who said that joy and sweetness are in the very words you
hear would be likely to say that this was like the way in which you

might also see an image in the very sentence which you hear—a bald head in the word "but." I should like in any case to try something different.

I do not intend to abandon the analogy with language yet. Music is expression of emotion as sentences are expression of ideas. But now how do sentences express ideas? We have noticed one way in which sentences do sometimes have meaning. Sentences, however, have been described in many ways. Sentences are like buzzers, like doorbells, like electric switches. Sentences are like mirrors, like maps, like pictures; sentences are like road signs, with arrows pointing the way. And so we might go on to ask, "Is music like buzzers, like pictures, like road sign arrows?" I do not however intend to do this. It will be noticed that the same analogy by which we have been trying to understand music, art, etc., may serve us also to understand what language is like. The analogy presupposes that we do know something about music, and so turning the analogy to this use may be fruitful. It might show us just how enlightening and how unenlightening the analogy is.

In order to study the analogy between music and the sentence and to try in this way to find out what the sentence is like, I now intend to offer a foolish theory. This may throw into clearer relief what Santayana says. What is understanding a sentence like? Understanding a sentence is speaking the sentence in a certain way. You can tell, listening to yourself talk, that you are understanding the sentence, and so can anyone else who hears you speak. Understanding has its rhythm. So the meaning of the sentence consists in a certain reading of the sentence. If, in this case, a sentence is spoken and not understood by someone, there would be only one thing to do, namely, speak the sentence again. Obviously this account will not do for there are other ways of clarifying what we mean. Nevertheless in some cases it may be all that is necessary.

Now notice. If this were what the meaning of a sentence is like, we should see at once what was meant if someone said that the meaning or the idea is in the sentence. For if there is meaning, where could it be but in the sentence, since the sentence is all there is. Of course, it is true that the sentence would have to be spoken and, of course, spoken in some way or other. And with every variation in reading it might then be said to have a different meaning. If anyone asked, "And what does the sentence mean?" expecting you to point to something or to elaborate the matter in gestures or to translate, it would be clear that he quite misunderstood what meaning is like. One might even correct him, saying it is even misleading to say that the meaning is in the sentence, as though it were only a part of the sentence, or tucked away somehow under overlapping syllables. A sentence having meaning in a case like this would be something like a living thing. Here too one might ask, "Where is the life in a squirrel and in a geranium?" Truly the life is the squirrel and is the geranium and is no part of either nor tucked away in some hidden fold or tiny vein. And so it is with the sentence, according to our imaginary theory. We might speak of the sentence as like a living thing.

And now let us see whether we have some corresponding use for "The joy and sweetness are in the very words you hear." People do ask about the meaning of poems and even about the meaning of music. Let us first of all say that the meaning is "the joy and sweetness," and the sadness. And where are these? In the very words you hear, and in the music. And now notice that what was admittedly a foolish theory in respect to sentences is not a foolish theory in respect to poems or music. Do you get the poem? Do you get the music? If you do not, pointing, gestures, translations will not help. (Understanding the words is presupposed.) There will be only one thing to do, namely, read the verses again, play the music once more. And what will the joy and sweetness and the sadness be like? They will be like the life in the living thing, not to be distinguished as some one part of the poem or music and not another part, or as some shadow that follows the sounded words or tones. "In the very words you hear," like the squirrel in fur!

I infer now that the analogy between the "joy and sweetness" in words and the meaning in sentences is misleading and is not likely to be helpful. The meaning of sentences is translatable, but the "meaning" of poems, of music is not. We have seen how this is so. There may, of course, be something in the sounding of all sentences which is analogous to the "joy and sweetness in the very words," but it is not the meaning of those sentences. And now this is an interesting consequence. It makes sense to ask, "What does the sentence express?" It expresses a meaning, of course, and you may have some way of showing what this is, without using the sentence to do so. But now it makes no sense to ask, "What does the poem express?" or "What does the music express?" We may say, if we like, that both are expressive, but we must beware of the analogy with language. And we may prevent the helpless searching in this case, by insisting that they "express" nothing, nothing at all.

And now let us review. My assumption has been that the expression theory is plagued with certain analogies that are not clearly distinguished, and none of which finally is helpful without being misleading. The first analogy is that in terms of which we commonly think of emotions. The second is that in terms of which we think of language, the doorbell view. Besides this there are two different types of experience that arise in connection with art. One of these types may be fairly well described by the analogy with doorbell language. The similarity of our language, however, in respect to both these types of experience, conceals the difference between those two types. Santayana's sentence reveals the agony that follows the recognition of this difference in these types of experience and the attempt to employ the language which describes the one to describe the other. The language requires very interesting translation. My conclusion, accordingly, is this: The analogy drawn from language may be useful in describing one type of experience. It is practically useless in describing the other. Since, then, these two analogies dominate the use of the word "expression," I suggest that, for the sake of clarity and charity, they be abandoned in seeking to describe that "expressiveness" which Santayana says constitutes "a beauty."

If we now abandon these analogies, are we also to abandon the use of the word "expression"? Not unless we please to do so. But we do so at our risk, for these analogies are not easily abandoned. We may, however, fortify our use of this word by considerations such as these. We use the word "expressive" to describe faces. And we use "expressive" in much the same way that we use the phrase "has character." A face that is expressive "has character." But when we now say that a face has character, this may remind us that the letters of the alphabet are characters. Let us suppose for a moment that this is related to "He's a character!" I suppose that he's a character and he has a character do not mean quite the same thing. There are antics in he's a character. Try again: The zig-zag line has character and the wavy line has character. Each letter of the alphabet is a character, but also has character. The number tokens, 1 2 3 4 5 6 7 8 9— each has its character. In the same way sounds have character. Let me see whether we can explain this further. You might say that if some dancing master were to arrange a dance for each of the numbers, you might see how a dance for the number one would not do at all for number five. Or again if the numbers were to be dressed in scarfs, again a certain color and a certain flimsy material would do for six but would not suit five at all. Now something of the same sort is true of words, and particularly of some. Words have character. I am tempted to say that all these things have their peculiar feel, but this then must be understood on the analogy with touch. If we, for instance, said that all these things have their peculiar feeling, then once again it might be supposed that in connection with them there is a feeling which is aroused by them.

Let your ears and your eyes, perhaps, too, feel these familiar bits of nonsense:

> Hi diddle diddle!
> Fee! fi, fo, fum!
> Intery, mintery.
> Abra ca da bra.

Each has its character. Each is, in this sense, expressive. But

to ask now "What is its character or what does it express?" is to
fall into the pit. You may, of course, experiment to exhibit more
clearly just what the character, in each case, is. You may, for
instance, contrast the leaping, the stomping, the mincing, the
shuffle, with what you get if you change the vowels. Try:

> Ho! doddle doodle!
> fa, fo, fu, fim!
> Untery, muntery.
> Ay bray cay day bray.

One might also go on to change consonants in order again to
exhibit character by giving the word new edges and making
their sides steeper or smoothing them down.

I do not intend, in proposing illustrations of this sort, to
suggest that art is nonsense and that its character is simple as
these syllables are. A face, no doubt may bear the impress, the
character, of a life's torment and of its hope and victory. So too
words and phrases may come blazing out of the burning past.
In art the world is born afresh, but the travail of the artist may
have had its beginnings in children's play. My only point is that
once the poem is born it has its character as surely as a cry in
the night or intery, mintery. And this character is not something
that follows it around like a clatter in a man's insides when he
reads it. The light of the sun is in the sun, where you see it. So
with the character of the poem. Hear the words and do not
imagine that in hearing them you gulp a jigger to make yourself
foam. Rather suppose that the poem is as hard as marble,
ingrained, it may be, with indelible sorrow.

If, accordingly, we now use the sentence "Art is expression,"
or "Art is expressive," and the use of this sentence is determined
by elucidations such as I have just now set out, then, I think,
that our language may save us from some torture. And this
means that we are now prepared to use freely those sentences
that the expression theory is commonly inclined to correct. For
now, unabashed, we shall say that the music is sad, and we shall
not go on to say that this means that the music expresses

sadness. For the sadness is to the music rather like the redness to the apple, than it is like the burp to the cider. And above all we shall not, having heard the music or read the poem, ask, " What does it express?"

IV.

And now it's many words ago since we left Verbo and his friend at the corner. Verbo was trying to figure out, you remember, how the music was related to his grandmother. How can music be sad? I suggested then that he was having word trouble, and that it would be necessary to probe his sentences. And so we probed. And now what shall we tell Verbo?

Verbo, we will say, the music is sad. And then we will remind him that the geranium is living, and that the sun is light. We will say these things so that he will not look away from the music to discover the sadness of it. Are you looking for the life in the geranium? Are you looking for the light in the sun? As then the life and the light describe the geranium and the sun, so too does sadness describe the music. And then we shall have to go on to tell him about these fearful analogies, and about Santayana's wrestle on the precipice. And about how we cut the ropes! And you may be sure that just as things are going along so well, Verbo will ask, flicking the ashes from his cigarette, "And what about the sadness?"

And now it's time to take the cat out of the bag, for so far all that has been exposed is the bag. The sadness is a quality of what we have already described as the character, the expressive. One piece of music is like and unlike some other pieces of music. These similarities and these differences may be perceived. Now then, we have a class of sad music. But why sad, that is, why use this word? It must be remembered, of course, that the use of this word is not precise. So there may be some pieces of music which are unmistakably sad, and others which shade off in gradations to the point where the question "Is it sad?" is not even asked. Suppose we ask our question "Why sad?" in respect to the unmistakable cases. Then, perhaps, some such answer as this will do. Sad music has some of the characteristics of people who are sad. It will be slow, not tripping: it will be low, not tinkling. People who are sad move more slowly, and when they speak, they speak softly and low. Associations of this sort may, of course, be multiplied indefinitely. And this now is the kitten in whose interest we made so much fuss about the bag. The kitten has, I think, turned out to be a scrawny little creature, not worth much. But the bag was worth it.

The bag was worth it? What I have in mind is that the identification of music as the expressive, as character, is crucial. That the expressive is sad serves now only to tag the music. It is introspective or, in relation to the music, an aside. It's a judgment that intervenes. Music need not be sad, nor joyous, nor anything else. Aestheticians usually account for this by inventing all sorts of emotions without names, an emotion for every piece of music. Besides, bad music, characterless music, the unexpressive, may be sad in quite the same way that good music may be. This is no objection, of course, to such classifications. I an interested only in clarifying the distinction between our uses of these several sentences.

And now that I have come to see what a thicket of tangle-words I've tried to find my way through, it seems to me that I am echoing such words as years ago I read in Croce, but certainly did not then understand. Perhaps if I read Croce again now I shouldn't understand them either. "Beauty is expression."

DESCARTES' SKEPTICISM OF THE SENSES

ONE OF THE MOST FAMOUS of all puzzles in the history of philosophy is that generated by Descartes' famous argument concerning the senses. The conclusion of that argument is skepticism of the senses generally. The central puzzle may be expressed in the question: "Am I awake or asleep?" I want in what follows to show how this puzzle is generated, and to show in what the puzzle consists.

The argument is this: "But it may be that although the senses sometimes deceive us concerning things which are hardly perceptible or very far away, there are yet many others to be met with as to which we cannot reasonably have any doubt, although we recognize them by their means. For example there is the fact that I am here, seated by the fire, attired in a dressing gown, having this paper in my hands, and other similar matters.....

"At the same time I must remember that I am a man, and that consequently I am in the habit of sleeping, and in my dreams representing to myself the same things or sometimes even less probable things, than do those who are insane in their waking moments. How often has it happened to me that in the night I dreamt that I found myself in this particular place, that I was dressed and near the fire, whilst in reality I was lying undressed in bed! At this moment it does indeed seem to me that it is with eyes awake that I am looking at this paper.... But in thinking over this I remind myself that on many occasions I have in sleep been deceived by similar illusions, and in dwelling carefully on this reflection I see so manifestly that there are no certain indications by which we may clearly distinguish wakefulness from sleep that I am lost in astonishment, and my astonishment is such that it is almost capable of persuading me that I now dream."[1]

Descartes is considering a certain class of perceptions, namely, those concerning which it may be said that with respect to them "we cannot reasonably have any doubt." This class is distinguished from those perceptions of things "hardly perceptible or very far away" with respect to which "the senses sometimes deceive us." Concerning perceptions in the latter class, I take it that Descartes is saying that with respect to any member of this class we may "reasonably" have a doubt. The reasonableness of the doubt in any such case is based on the fact that the perceiver in question will in the past have been deceived in some perceptions of this class. Hence every member of that class is now under suspicion. Now it may be that with respect to any member of the first class, we may also have reasonable doubts, and for the same sort of reason, namely that one has at some time or other been deceived. Descartes might have said: Just as you once mistook a cow out there beyond the meadow for a pony, and so you cannot trust your eyes in distinguishing far away things, so too I remember your flicking your ashes into a bowl of soup which you mistook for an ash tray, and so you cannot trust your eyes to distinguish things near-by either. But Descartes does not say this. He does, of course, say that concerning the bowl of soup you may also have a reasonable doubt, but not because you have ever been deceived about a bowl or an ash tray. I want to notice closely just what in such cases does, according to Descartes, constitute the basis of a reasonable doubt.

[1] *Philosophical Works of Descartes*, trans. E. S. Haldane and G. R. T. Ross (2 vols.; Cambridge: Cambridge University Press, 1912), I, 145–146.

Before I proceed, I should like to point out with respect to Descartes' argument, that if it is a good argument, it remains a good argument even though no man at any time has been deceived by the senses. The argument does not depend in any way upon any instance of deception. It's as though Descartes asked: And do the senses deceive us? To which the answer is: Never. He goes on: Are the senses then to be trusted? to which he answers: Certainly not. This illustrates the unusual character of his argument. It may be noticed too that if his argument holds for that class of perceptions by which we perceive things near-by, it holds equally for that class of perceptions by which we perceive "things hardly perceptible and far-away." No perception is to be trusted.

We have then to consider what fact it is, about all perceptions whatsoever, that constitutes a basis for reasonable doubt concerning any perception. Descartes starts out from what he describes as a fact. "...there is *the fact that* I am here, seated by the fire, attired in a dressing gown, having this paper in my hands, and other similar matters." It is important to recognize that this is introduced as a fact. Concerning this Descartes has no doubt, either reasonable or unreasonable. In contrast with this Descartes now recollects certain dreams of his. "How often has it happened to me that in the night I dreamt that I found myself in this particular place, that I was dressed, and near the fire, whilst in reality I was lying undressed in bed." Concerning this Descartes is also quite certain. These were only dreams. There are here then two facts which provide Descartes with the starting point of his argument. There is the fact "I am here,... etc.," and there is the fact that I dreamed that I was here, "seated by the fire... etc." It may be odd that Descartes should have dreamed what actually often happened, and odder still that he should have dreamed this often. If one is inclined to any reasonable doubt concerning this, at any rate one may admit all that is requisite to the argument. All that is necessary is that Descartes should have dreamed it once.

We might even admit that once upon a time Descartes was

"here, seated by the fire, attired in a dressing gown, having this paper in (his) hands," and that he fell asleep and dreamed. And Descartes dreamed, and behold! he dreamed that he was "here, seated by the fire, attired in a dressing gown, having this paper in (his) hands." Descartes, having dreamed, awoke, and he recollected his dream, and it was so.

Now what strikes Descartes is the likeness of the fact to what he has dreamed. The description of the fact is identical with the description of what he dreamed. This disturbs Descartes, and the disturbance is obvious in the language which he now employs. "At this moment it does indeed seem to me that it is with eyes awake that I am looking at this paper...." The assumption is, of course, that if it only seems "that it is with eyes awake," then, too, it only seems "that I am here, seated by the fire...." The alleged fact from which the argument proceeded has begun to shake. But so far as I can see there is no corresponding concretion, substantiation, of the dream. The real shakes, but the dream remains a dream. There is no exchange of status. Descartes does not say: Well, maybe what I took to be the fact is a dream, and what I took to be a dream is the fact. It is the fact which dissolves under this inspection. Maybe everything is dreams. Curiously, however, dreams are still described as deceiving "by similar illusions." But in this case, what is deception and what is illusion?

I should like now to study this predicament more closely. Imagine yourself in a fixed position in relation to a garden and to a mirror reflecting that garden as perfectly as possible. Imagine further that the mirror is not distinguishable. There is no shimmer, no smoothly shining surface. Now then suppose further that before you were placed in this position you thought you knew which was the garden and which was the reflection, but immediately before you were placed in that position you were turned round and round, and made so dizzy that even when you had recovered you were unable to identify which was the garden and which was the reflection. Now the question is put to you: Which is the garden, and which is the reflection?

And you must answer by way of inspection from that fixed position. You look, and bend your head, now this way, now that; you study the detail of each closely, but all in vain. By inspection you cannot make out which is which. If by this time you have recollected somehow, which of the two you would have identified as the garden, had you not previously been made dizzy, you may also have lost all confidence in your previous judgment. "It did indeed seem to me that that was the garden, but in thinking over this I can see how a mirror reflection may have deceived me." If you are bold these possibilities may now occur to you:

(a) One is a garden and one is a reflection, but there is no way of knowing which is which.

(b) There are two gardens.

(c) There are two reflections.

You may, of course, conclude that hunches are from God, and that God's hunches are good hunches. So you had better try to discover your hunch.

Now this is something like the predicament in which Descartes finds himself. He sets out confidently enough from "the fact that I am here" (the garden), and the dream that I am here (the reflection). But too much inspection, or the wrong question prompting the inspection, dizzies him. He loses his confidence. Is this the fact? How does one tell? It seems to me that this is the fact, but that other too seems to me to be the fact. If only facts were marked F and what is merely dreamed marked D, everything would be so simple. As it is there is no telling. There are in any case three possibilities:

(a) One is fact and one is dream.

(b) Both are facts.

(c) Both are dreams.

Descartes sets out confidently from (a), but loses that confidence, and relapses into (c). Curiously it does not occur to Descartes to suggest that both are facts.

I want now to trace the course of his loss of confidence. The facts involved, and the nature of Descartes' probing are clear enough. Just where now does the dizziness begin?

Let us recollect Descartes begins with "the fact that I am here, seated by the fire, etc." Now he asks: But am I here, seated by the fire? His response is: "At this moment it does indeed seem to me that it is with eyes awake that I am looking over this paper." Clearly Descartes thinks that if he can be sure that he is awake, then he can be sure that he is here, seated by the fire. Very well then: Am I awake? I can't tell. How can I tell? Well, if it seems to me that I am here and I really am here, then I am awake. But am I here? That is the question. Since now the only fact which remains is that it seems to me that I am here, and that fact is equally established for any case in which I dream that I am here, there is no way of telling whether I am awake or dreaming. "There are no certain indications by which we may clearly distinguish wakefulness from sleep." It follows, of course, that Descartes cannot tell whether he is here, seated by the fire, etc., or not. One might in play suggest that he try going to bed and try falling asleep. If he succeeds, he was awake, and then it will follow that he was here.

Now I want to notice the peculiar question which Descartes asks himself: Am I awake or am I asleep? This question is either a very peculiar question or it is readily answerable. In order to exhibit this I want to consider certain other questions which are very much like this.

Let us consider the question: Is he awake or asleep? We know very well how to go about finding out. Let us suppose he is lying down on a couch. Tip-toe up to him. Listen. You can tell by his breathing. Is he snoring lightly maybe? Is he talking incoherently perhaps as men do in their sleep? Look at him. Are his eyes open? Does he follow you with his eyes as you walk? Does he snuggle his head lower into the covers to avoid you as you approach? Are there lines on his cheek? Is his mouth open? Are there pouches under his eyes? Still you cannot tell? Well, talk to him, then, tell him his dinner is served or set the alarm clock at his head, and see how he re-acts. If you are still undecided, wait and when he gets up, ask him whether he was asleep. We know certainly how to find out whether he is asleep or not. And the same thing is true whether we ask as to whether he is now asleep or whether he was asleep.

We also have a use for the question: Are you awake? If one is awake, one may answer. The answer may then be "yes." If it turns out to be "no," there will be something suspicious about the answer. The "no" may be equivalent to yes, but I won't tell you, or may be uttered in sleep in which case the tone of the utterance may give evidence. In any case if the respondent is awake, he asks himself, "Am I awake?" and then gives the answer. I suppose that this is misleading actually. He does not ask himself since he knows and is not even curious. He simply is aware of what you want to know. On the other hand if he is asleep, your question is to be treated in the same way in which the question: Is he awake? was treated. Your asking the question, "Are you awake?" may serve in the way in which any other question or remark would serve. If there is no response or a sleepy one, then he is asleep, and you have the desired information.

The questions: Is he awake? and Are you awake? are accordingly readily intelligible. Now consider the question: Am I awake? There are certain kinds of experience, I think, in which this question is also intelligible. There is a rhetorical use of this expression with which we are all familiar, but in this use it is, of course, no longer a question. It serves in this instance simply to express one's usually grateful surprise. If today, walking along your street, you were to meet Mr. Stalin and you were at the moment convinced that this was Mr. Stalin, you might not then, as we say, believe your eyes. Your words might then be: Can this be? Am I awake or is this a dream? Your words would be Cartesian but your astonishment would be of a quite ordinary sort.

But there are also cases in which for a minute or for an

instant we are genuinely puzzled and do ask: Am I awake or am I dreaming? There are experiences of waking out of a dream where the vivid peril of one's dream has not yet passed and when the safety of the real world is not yet clear, in which one may quite earnestly and fearfully and hopefully ask: Am I awake or dreaming? Then with great relief one may pat the pillow underneath one's head and greet the security of dawning light through the window. Such a question may indeed be asked with fear and trembling, and here too, fortunately, we also know how to distinguish the pit and the pendulum of our dreams from the refuge of a real bed and dear space. But notice that the question arises only when there is an awareness both of the strange encounter in the dream, and of something else vaguely distinguished in contrast with that encounter, and more definitely defined as one finds relief in one's answer. The identification of the pillow and of the familiar light through the window serve also to identify the horrors of the dream. It's like coming home after a journey, and enjoying the scene of one's habitual comfort.

There are no doubt other experiences, experiences of hallucination and delirium, in which we can well imagine questions very much like this. Macbeth's question:

> Is this a dagger which I see before me,
> The handle towards my hand?...
> . . . .
> Art thou not, fatal vision, sensible
> To feeling as to sight? or art thou but
> A dagger of the mind, a false creation,
> Proceeding from the heat-oppressed brain?

is of this sort. Am I suffering an hallucination, or is this a real dagger? But once more the question is to be understood as arising from Macbeth's own recognition of a strangeness in this apparition in contrast with the familiar order of the furnishings of his affairs. And he makes up his mind in a moment:

> . . . . . There's no such thing.

Macbeth does not treat the question as a philosophical puzzle.

If he had, of course, there would have been no play. Had Macbeth cogitated further and concluded with: "At this moment it does indeed seem to me that it is with eyes awake that I am looking at this dagger.... But...," he would not have murdered sleep.

We are now prepared to examine Descartes' question: Am I awake or am I asleep? What prompts the question is first of all nothing like what prompts the question in any of these other cases. It isn't because he is lying down in a posture suitable to sleep that he becomes curious about himself, as though he wanted, for instance, to know so that he would not disturb himself with any noise. It isn't either that he has been asleep and has dreamed and has not fully recovered the assurance of his return to the substantial springs and mattress under him and the blue ceiling over him. There is no present fading dream, and no present emerging real world. And, of course, there is no vision, fatal or otherwise, that puzzles him. What, then, provokes the question? Nothing but the awareness of a certain fact, namely, that one may have dreamed something very much like what one now perceives to be the fact.

Now let us try the question in the ordinary sense to see how Descartes might have gotten on with it. Either now Descartes is awake or he is asleep. Let us suppose first of all that he is awake. He is awake, sitting before the fire, etc., and he asks himself with a perfectly serious face: Am I awake? The question seems a little foolish, but let us treat it as though it were not foolish. By analogy with the question: Is he awake? he may try out the suggestions above. He may ask: Are my eyes closed? Am I snoring? Is my breathing like that of one asleep? etc. To all of these questions his answer is: No. Now if he is still uneasy he may call the landlady and ask her these questions. What she can discover will also be evidence. There is, in any case, no reason why Descartes could not answer his question. There is no puzzle. But if this will still not do, he may try the kinds of questions which the man waking from a dream tries: Is this the one-armed chair I always sit awake in? Of course. Is that the fireplace I throw twigs in? Throw a twig in. See it burn. If I shout will the landlady come in to bring me tea? Do. She did. And so on. It's the same old world, furnished with the same pleasant useful things. I am awake! Oh joy! Descartes is awake, and he knows it in the way in which we do discover facts of this kind.

Now let us suppose that Descartes is asleep. Now he asks: Am I asleep? It must be remembered, of course, that if he asks this, and is asleep, that he must be asking this in a dream, and must be asking this about what he is dreaming of. Accordingly he must be dreaming of himself as either awake or dreaming. But now obviously the nature of the test will not be different from the case in which he asked the question, being awake. Hence if Descartes is clearheaded as he asks the question and sets out in his dream to examine the Descartes he is dreaming of, that Descartes must furnish the evidence. Are his eyes open? Is he snoring? etc. We need not rehearse the nature of the relevant evidence. Everything depends upon the use of the expressions: Am I awake or asleep? and that one asks, being awake or asleep, will make no difference at all. It is clear then that if Descartes were using these expressions as they are ordinarily used, there is no reason why he should not readily find the answer to his question.

What I am mainly interested in pointing out is precisely that Descartes' use of the expression: Am I awake or asleep? is not ordinary, and that his own unresolved puzzlement arises from this fact. The explanation is, I think, simple. It will be noticed that in all these common uses of this expression, the context in which the question arises involves the distinction of the real world, what Descartes introduced originally as the fact that I am here, etc. The question: Is he asleep? presupposes the real bulk of him prone on the couch, with eyes closed, a loose mouth, snoring facility, couch, pillow, etc.? The question: Am I awake? in the same way presupposes the familiar scene to be recognized, one's long snuggled pillow, the window and the peering light at the left, the swish of elm boughs outside, the screen, etc.

How does Macbeth intend to test "the false creation"? By getting his hands on it. He is sure enough of his hands. His hands are not the stuff that dreams are made of. This, then, the real world, furnishes the criteria by which waking and sleeping are determined.

Doesn't Descartes then know all this? When Descartes asks: Am I awake? doesn't he know that open eyes are an indication that he is awake? Yes, he knows. This isn't news to him. He says "it does indeed seem to me that it is with eyes awake...." The trouble now is that he cannot tell whether his eyes are open or not. True, they seem to be open, but that is not enough. Why then doesn't he throw a twig in the fire, finger his dressing gown, call the landlady? This won't help. For, for any test proposed, it will call forth the same story. "It does indeed seem to me" that I throw a chip on the fire, that this is my dressing gown, my fingers, and that the landlady said: Why, of course, Etienne (she never got my name right), your eyes are open. Clearly Descartes has abandoned the original distinction, the fact that I am here, etc., and the fact that I dreamed that I am here, etc., upon the basis of which he elaborated his argument. In order to find out whether he is awake or not, he must depend upon facts of the sort he began with. He continues however to use language which is significant only in terms of the distinctions which he has abandoned. The questions "Am I awake?" "Am I asleep?" are questions about bodies. Since he has ruled out bodies as within the range of the application of these terms, his language is now meaningless.

Had Descartes asked the question: Am I alive? or Am I dead? the same difficulty would have become evident. Am I alive? Feel of your heart. Breathe over a mirror. Walk. Talk. Still Descartes cannot tell. Why not? Because he cannot get at his heart. Mirrors are always behind seemings, and Descartes can never break through. He appears to walk and seems to talk, but real walking and talking are, if they are, beyond the veil. If Descartes had asked: Do I seem to be alive? he might very well have answered that question, but in the former case too he did not ask: Do I seem to be awake? or more precisely: Does the seeming I, seem to be awake? Here is another way of getting at the point. Descartes asks: Am I awake? The expression "awake" we have discussed. Now what does " I " apply to? If it applies to body, then the question presupposes what Descartes intends not to assert, namely the existence of body. But in that case, as has been pointed out above, the question can be answered easily enough. If on the other hand it refers not to body but to the self or mind, thinking substance, then what are the criteria of waking and sleeping thinking substances? Either the expressions employed here have no application, or once more the answers are easily forthcoming. Is a waking thinking substance, one which is active, asking such a question as: Am I awake? If so, Descartes is awake.

Descartes declared that he was lost in astonishment, and this is equivalent to saying that he was both lost and astonished. He writes as though he was lost because, the facts being what they are, he was incapable of distinguishing what he perceived and what was really so, from what he merely dreamed. Actually his starting point refutes this explanation. If Descartes was lost, this is rather because in thinking about "the fact" and his dream, he was misled into employing language under conditions stipulated by his own misgivings, such that the language so employed ceased to have any meaning. And this language is in this instance sufficient to give anyone a whirl. For the language itself is not at all suspicious. It is simple, ordinary language. "Am I awake or am I asleep?" But the condition defines the question in such a way that you must answer the question without employing the senses at all. You must not look or listen or ask anyone any questions. You must not suppose that there is any body to examine. Did the man commit murder? Oh, yes. And the body? There was none.

In what precedes, I have tried to discover what it is in Descartes' argument that makes it seem so convincing and yet convinces no one. My discovery then is this: What is crucial in the language of the argument has, by way of Descartes' philosophical misgiving, been cut off from all significance. Until this is understood, it may seem that Descartes' predicament is a predicament of ignorance, that he actually does not know whether he is awake or asleep. Once it is understood, however, one may also understand one's weakness, one's wilting, before this ghost question: Am I awake or am I asleep? and having recognized the ghost one may say: Booh! Then one may sit by the fire and twirl the tassels of one's dressing gown in confidence. It must be remembered that I have not dealt with the larger subject, skepticism of the senses. I have confined myself to a study of Descartes' argument.

VARIATIONS ON A THEME BY
MR. COSTELLO

"THE OLD LADY who saw the little kangaroo look out of the big kangaroo's pocket said quite naturally, 'Good heavens, what will they think of next.'"[1]

I said: "Lady, did you think 'they' thought up that pocket?"

She said: "I guess that's what I thought."

I said: "Lady, you're wrong."

She said: "But look at the fit of it, the snug of it."

I said: "Oh, yes. It's the means, all right."

At this point we examined the pocket, fur-lined, seamless, deep and roomy. I sank my right hand into it. It was marvelous, a little gay home in the vest. I even felt of the little pocket of the little kangaroo, a pocket edition of the original.

The old lady was shaking her head with admiration. She said: "But you said it was means?"

"Oh, yes," I said. "It's like the branches of trees that make lovely perches for birds to rest on, and like soft earth that moles hump up with tunnels. The branches are obviously means and so is the soft earth. So are sunshine and rain and seasons and moonshine."

"And are there ends too?"

[1] "The Naturalism of Woodbridge" by H. T. Costello, in *Naturalism and the Human Spirit*, ed., Y. H. Krikorian (New York: Columbia University Press, 1944).

"Of course. The birds want to rest, and the moles want to worm their way along."

"You say that they want to? I suppose their wanting to rest and their wanting to tunnel, is what makes these ends? Ends are what X's have in mind to do before they do what they do, and then look around for means, means such as branches and soft fields of earth? Curious. You know, I never thought of birds and moles as ever thinking at all of what they were to do. I can see in that case too how it is that the branches and the soft earth are convenient and adaptable to these ends; it is not all clear that 'they' thought up branches of trees for the birds and soft earth for the moles. It rather appears that the branches and the soft earth just happen to be there."

"Well, lady, I am glad you understand this. After this you won't be admiring the kangaroo's pocket and exclaiming about the ingenuity of the Great Tailor. The pocket of the kangaroo is as accidental to the kangaroo as the branches of the tree to the bird and as the soft earth to the mole."

She was a bit puzzled at this, and was silent. I could see that she was not convinced, and she was knitting her brows as though she might be trying her ingenuity to catch me up in some pocket of hers. Finally she said: "So you think that the pocket is to the kangaroo as the branch of the tree is to the bird? Strange! When I see birds carrying about with them collapsible trees to plant for perching at the end of their flights, then I will see how that is something like the case of the pocket, not draping the world at chance hopping intervals, to the kangaroo. As it is, I am a little bit puzzled. I had, of course, heard of people who say that kangaroos, birds, and moles, and people themselves too, are nicely adapted, but again without anyone's having 'thought' up the arrangement, to scientific method. They call this the brute fact, and brute it is. But once you admit ends, and then find a kangaroo with a pocket, that's very much like finding a can of sardines with a key attached for winding off the seal. 'Good heavens, what will they think of next.'"

At this point I was a bit upset by her being so natural. I was about to quote Dewey, and then I thought of Sidney Hook, but she kept looking at the kangaroo, and I made up my mind that as long as she did that there was no use. She would, I felt sure, keep harping on this built-in feature so easily suggesting pockets in dashboards of automobiles and cubbies in kitchens, etc. And I was fearing all the time now that she would discover that the striking aspect of the kangaroo's pocket arises simply from its unusual character, and not at all from its admitted means service to some end. She might begin to think about hands and feet and ears and eyes and teeth. Would I then have to maintain that, though there are ends (of course, there are!), there are no means at all especially adapted to those ends? I felt sure all the time about the branches and about the soft earth, but I could not make my point clear about that pocket. It was a *cul de sac*.

"Lady," I said, "I think we have made a mistake. I will ask my brothers about this."

"Oh, don't go," she begged. "I seem to be taken in by this pocket. You know since you admitted ends, I can't understand your denying specially-prepared means. Now this arrangement here, closely woven into the slip-cover of this kangaroo, certainly suggests des——"

At this I could scarcely restrain myself and I came near shouting: "Lady, hush! The horrid word!"

She smiled. My taboo amused her.

Then she went on, "Design. Notice that it's precisely in the right place. The little kangaroo can not fall out, and it's just about properly centered to balance the weight of the kangaroo between the muscles on this side and on that," pointing to the left and right as the beast with rooful eyes wondered at all the fuss.

I was alternately incredulous (I could scarcely imagine that a woman who could observe, save data, and hypothesize, would say such things) and disgusted. But I did not leave. She continued: "Now if a kangaroo were covered with lappets and shreds and loops and furbelows, entangling the poor thing in trappings, then no doubt I should exclaim at the mess. Or if there were pockets of many sizes and in many positions, or if pockets were full of holes, and dropped little kangaroos and cocoanuts and cantaloupes like a colander, then again I should shake my head. I'd say: 'No means; no ends either.' Or if the kangaroo had a pocket on its head, and the little kangaroo climbed into it and tried to balance itself in the pocket on the kangaroo's head, and as soon as the mother kangaroo took even a tiny hop, the little kangaroo went spilling out, and lay there bruised on a stone, I'd once more remark upon the inconvenience, and the lack of economic planning. But it really isn't like that."

I said: "No, it isn't." Her use of that last phrase, economic planning, pleased me. I felt as though I was in the right company.

Nevertheless I was not exactly comfortable. I felt, indeed, rather helpless, reflecting upon her lack of scientific outlook. I was like a wanderer in time come suddenly upon a middle-ages mind in an old lady, more naïve than Aristotle. A kangaroo's pocket a design! Some things, I realized, which people say "quite naturally" are not and ought never to be allowed ever to be said. It was not encouraging. I was glad that neither Mr. Dewey nor Mr. Hook was with me. It would have upset them terribly.

She continued. "Now you say that there are ends—is it kangaroo ends?—and means. But, of course, no designed (ugh!) means. The pocket, for instance, is a means, but 'they' never thought it up. It's admitted that the pocket is adaptable, oh how adaptable! like the limb of a tree and soft earth, to the end, but it is not designed. What puzzles me now is this: Do you by examination of the pocket find this out? Isn't it complicated enough? Suppose, for instance, that in the pocket were other pockets in the lining of the larger pocket. And suppose that in those pockets were the materials of an emergency kit, fell vials of ointment, membrane sacs of dextro-maltose, tiny tubes of paw lotion—would an arrangement such as this lead you to say that there was design? Or suppose it carried there a miniature telephone-by-air, a simple hoppie-talkie, built right into the hop-board, would that convince you?"

I blushed.

"You know," she went on, "when you said that there were ends, it seemed to me that this must mean that the kangaroo might conceive of something it wanted, such as, for instance, being at a certain place and eating a banana. But then it occurred to me that if it could conceive of ends it might quite as well conceive of means. There is no difference, I take it, in the conceiving. And further, I thought, if it can execute the end proposed, why should it not conceive a means and make an end of it. Of course, maybe when you spoke of ends you were not really thinking of the kangaroo at all. Blake spoke, you remember, of nobodaddy and I said 'they.' Maybe you have a word for it. Certainly you do not mean that there are ends, but they are not the ends of nobodaddy nor of the kangaroo. It's just *als ob* you didn't mean what you said."

She looked at me and then she looked at the kangaroo. As a matter of fact she winked at the kangaroo, and the kangaroo bumped the little kangaroo out of the pocket, and then the kangaroo stuck her paw in her pocket, and perkily waited. The little kangaroo fell up and around, practicing hopping.

I was glad for the interruption and laughed, but the old lady was not finished. She resumed: "I think I know what you might say. Once upon a long time ago the kangaroos had no pockets at all. The weather was warm. In fact it was a hot time and the little kangaroos lay sprawling by day and by night or they hippetied along when moving time came. There was not a sneeze in a generation. But all the while there was a cycle and soon cold was all over the hopping-range. The little kangaroos shivered. Of course they gravitated toward their warm mothers. ('Gravitated' is a good word.) Having gravitated, however, they were still not very warm, and they tried then to tiny-paw their ways into their mother's fur. (As you know, Mr. Freud did not forget to notice this.) The first little kangaroos did not do very well. With the little impressions they made in their mothers, it's a miracle (pardon me!) that they were not nipped right off by some of those keen airs. But they lived. Anyhow the ninety degrees of that cycle was a billion days or years or geological ages in moderating. When it was all over, what do you suppose?

No, you're wrong. It's hard to believe, I know, but behold! there was the kangaroo with a pocket, jaunty as a mailman with his pouch. And the pocket was admirably suited to cradle and cozy the little kangaroo, and convenient too for travel. And that is how the kangaroo got its pocket. Is this the sort of thing you mean? By the way, someday I should like too to tell you how the elephant got its howdah."

I said: "Lady, I said ends and means but that's as far as I can go." I think I stamped my foot, and suffered a mutation of one of my natural selection toes. And now I did leave, relieved to have kept my naturalistic integrity (a little stretched, I know), and to have saved my soul. My what? Confound that woman!

NATURALISM*

I SHOULD LIKE first of all to state as precisely as I can that proposition or those propositions with which in part, at least, naturalism is to be identified. For this purpose, I should like to take sentences straight out of the test tube—a much more authentic source even than the horse's mouth. Once having identified these sentences, I intend to examine them in order to discover further how to deal with them. Are the sentences in question exclamatory, or empirical, or are they tautologies?

The sentences which I am to quote are sentences in which their authors, respectively, aim to define naturalism. These sentences fall into two groups, and the distinction between them will immediately be evident. Here now are three in the first group. The first is from Edel. Here it is: "Reliance on scientific method together with an appreciation of the primacy of matter, and the pervasiveness of change, I take to be the central points of naturalism as a philosophic outlook." [1] The second is from Hook: "What unites them all is the whole-hearted acceptance of scientific method as the only reliable way of reaching truth about the world, nature, society, and man. The

* Read at a symposium on "The Present Status of Naturalism" at the meeting of the Western Division of the American Philosophical Association, Iowa City, May 9, 1947.

[1] *Naturalism and the Human Spirit*, ed. Y. H. Krikorian (New York: Columbia University Press, 1944), p. 63.

least common denominator of all historic naturalisms, therefore, is not so much a set of specific doctrines as the method of scientific or rational empiricism." [2] The third is from Dewey; it runs: "It suffices here to note that the naturalist is one who has respect for the conclusions of natural science." [3]

Now these three sentences agree in identifying naturalism with a certain attitude toward scientific method, variously described as "reliance upon," "whole-hearted acceptance of," and "respect for." Every naturalist is one who maintains an attitude similar to the attitude here described. He is excited about something. The excitement may vary in intensity, but in some degree naturalists all share it. This is not difficult to understand. In many cases, no doubt such excitement is the spontaneous overflow of new curiosities looking forward to tomorrow. There are secrets in 10,000 boxes, and you have opened forty, and know now how to go on opening a box a day for the rest of your life. What a feast for eager eyes! Who has not shaken a box and wondered, keyless, what was inside it—and later, furnished with a key, found out? Precious key! Well, a naturalist is a man with 10,000 unopened boxes, newly furnished with a key. No wonder he dances, key in hand up-raised, among the boxes.

But this is idle curiosity, idle secrets for idle eyes, and is only half the motive of the naturalists' dance. For in those boxes snuggled away out of men's sight is the furniture of the land of hearts' desire. Here is a box of the beauty that will not fade in the rain. Here is a heart that will not fail, a pump with scrutable controls. Here are pellets for stretching the hours, and wobbling all dimensions. Here are new snuffers for old pains and here are new pleasures for old duffers. Besides, there are new and quick get-aways, new smashers, new glue better than love, daisies that will tell even what the old ones wouldn't, rapid transit swifter than *gloria mundi*, lightning to keep your orange-juice cold, falling water to dry your feet, shocks to give you peace, a drop or two to make you jump, babies delivered in cellophane,

[2] *Ibid.*, p. 45.   [3] *Ibid.*, p. 2.

bloodless wars, holocaust by button, one big rumble for all last "whimpers," a piece of powder for a gland, teeth from Dupont's, everlasting shoes, a feather to lighten your load, suspenders to keep up your courage, a new Joseph for all your dreams, cant about what man can, the last straw, and so on from 9,000 and more other boxes. So the naturalist does his dazzle dance. Who then would not accept scientific method, and prefer to go to Babylon by candle-light? Scientific method is successful.

So far then there is no issue, no controversy, and by that token we may be sure that we have not yet ventured to be philosophical. Be reminded, then, of what so far we missed and be prepared to resist. Mr. Hook speaks of "the whole-hearted acceptance of scientific method as the only reliable way of reaching truth." And now we are prepared to introduce that second group of sentences. In this group are these sentences: The first from Dennes, which is this: "There is for naturalism no knowledge except of the type ordinarily called scientific,"[4] and this one from Krikorian: "For naturalism as a philosophy, the universal applicability of the experimental method is a basic belief."[5] By the pricking of the hair on your chinny chin chin I realize that these are philosophic statements.

Let us now consider these sentences, with special attention to the phrases: "the only reliable way," "no knowledge except," "the universal applicability of." Obviously the point of such sentences is that other men have spoken of "other reliable ways," of "knowledge other than," of "a certain inapplicability." Notice first the form of Dennes's sentence. Mr. Ringling might say: "There is for Ringling Brothers no elephant except of the type ordinarily called big." Does Mr. Ringling intend to deny there are any little elephants? Does he mean that besides Jumbo and Mumbo there is no little Nimblo? I think he means no more than that there is a difference between big elephants and little elephants, and that Mr. Ringling has no use for little elephants. If you tried to sell him one, he wouldn't buy. He can't use any. Or try this sentence: "For all the boys in our

[4] *Ibid.*, p. 289.   [5] *Ibid.*, p. 242.

alley, there's no girl but pretty Sally." What, have the boys in our alley seen no girl but pretty Sally? Don't be silly. Of course, they know Helen and Ruth and Betty. It's just a way of saying that above all the girls they know, they prefer Sally.

And this is now the way in which we are to understand Mr. Dennes? Does he mean to be stating a preference? Mr. Ringling says: "There are really no elephants but big ones," and the boys in our alley say: "There's really no girl but Sally." So Mr. Dennes: "There's really no knowledge but...." In this case, of course, Mr. Dennes might have admitted other types of knowledge too, but would in this instance merely have intended to say: "Well, so long as I have my choice, let mine be scientific." In this case, once more there would be no issue. If Mr. Dennes prefers blondes or gas-heat or lemonade, or a hard mattress or scientific knowledge, well, that's all there is to it. I think that this is certainly something like what Dennes is saying, but not quite.

Before we settle these matters, let us inspect Krikorian's sentence. It is: "For naturalism as a philosophy, the universal applicability of the experimental method is a basic belief." Consider the parallel sentence of the vacuum cleaner salesman: "For vacuumism as a philosophy, the universal applicability of the suction nozzle is a basic belief." He may argue to himself: "If I ever give this up, I'll never sell another vacuum cleaner. It is basic." To the house-wife who asks: "And can you use it to dust books?" he replies: "Of course." And when he shows her and finds that it does not do so well, does he deny the universal applicability of the nozzle? No such thing. He may complain that he himself is not skillful, or that what seems like dust to the house-wife is not dust. The universal applicability of the nozzle is now the touchstone of dust. If the nozzle is applicable, it's dust. If it is not applicable, it is not dust. Is Krikorian's statement now like the statement of the vacuum-cleaner salesman? Well, for the moment, I should like to say that it is, and then to add, before I breathe, that it isn't. And for the next moment I should like to postpone my decision.

It will be remembered that at the outset I proposed to determine whether the sentences defining naturalism were exclamatory, or empirical, or tautologies. I think, though I have made no point of it, that naturalists are very fervent. But I also think now that without further trial of these sentences it will be misleading to classify them in either way. I propose accordingly to dandle them some more before deciding. Let us, then, just playfully bounce them.

There are, in any case, at least three ways of frisking a philosophical theory. You may try to misunderstand it which in philosophy requires almost no effort at all. Almost anyone can at once misunderstand a philosophical statement. This method is very popular, very chuckling, but also very exasperating. In any case I have already forsworn the obvious advantages of this and must resort to something else. Fortunately there are other ways. You may then in the second place try to refute the theory in question. In this case you settle upon some clear and plausible import of the theory, and then you discover some contradiction. The contradiction must be hidden, subtle, and for the best results should pop out like a jack-in-the-box. You show that the theory conceals a jack-in-the-theory, which the theory on its face denied. The theory said: "No, no, there's no little jack," and then you pressed a little word, and out popped jack. This method is ideal, absolutely ruinous, guaranteed to fluster. Every philosopher submits to it with modesty, and, after three minutes, with cheers, whenever, that is, he also recognizes the little jack. The most authentic and last case of this sort is, as you will remember, recorded with a new-fangled pen in the reminiscences of a certain Thales whose comment on this has amused many scholars since. His comment is, "Of this too it may be said that all is wet." There is a third method which is this. You may try to understand the theory in question. This is, of course, a very dangerous expedient. It is clear that having understood the theory you may be taken in by it, and so suffer the corruption which you certainly intended at the outset to avoid. On the other hand you may discover that what you have come to understand turns out now to be so trivial that all your effort can scarcely be dignified by the admission. It's quite all right to leap bravely from one's horse to let the blood of a wind-mill, so long as you can keep on calling the wind-mill Beelzebub. But who would fence with a piece of wood? So the risk is great. There are, however, rewards. A little corruption will no doubt improve everyone.

And now I should like to try the second of these methods, refu-tation. And let us settle without very nice circumspection upon this sentence: "Only scientific method is successful." Can this sentence be refuted?

Now there certainly are people who think that it can be refuted. These refutations take at least two forms. There are first of all people who argue in this way. They say: "The application of scientific method, whatever it is, does involve thinking. Now thinking itself pre-supposes certain facts, namely, the laws of thought. For the truth of these laws there can be no evidence, for any evidence at all would once again pre-suppose them. Hence, since we obviously do know these laws, there obviously is knowledge, other than knowledge arrived at by scientific method." Nor is this all. It is clear that without the application of mathematics, scientific method would have been almost impotent. Now then, mathematics is also knowledge, and it is not commonly maintained even by those who are so excited by scientific method that there is anything experimental about mathematics. Once more, then, there is a type of knowledge, namely, mathematics—ask any mathematician whether he knows mathematics. And this is not knowledge which in any way depends upon scientific method. Both of these considerations seem so obvious that it is very curious there should be naturalists at all. Doesn't the naturalist then know, has he never heard, about the laws of thought and about numbers?

Of course he does and has, and yet he does not admit the refutation. What, then, does he say? Well, bluntly, that what in the proposed refutation is cited as knowledge, is not knowledge at all. There are logicians and there are mathematicians, but in these capacities they are not Knowers. The question here is as to what leads naturalists to speak so curiously, and then, once we have understood this, the further question is whether or not there still remains some intelligible issue as between the naturalist and his refuter. I am not at all certain now that I can represent this matter correctly, but I will do my best. Suppose we admit that knowledge is always about something or other. So if we know that thunder follows lightning, then what we know is something described by that sentence, and not at all to be identified with that sentence. We all know what this means. Now suppose we ask: "Do the laws of thought describe anything? Is that they do not, what you mean by their being laws? Further does $2+2=4$ describe something?" If you hesitate over these questions, then I think that you have some inkling as to what the naturalist here has in mind. That thunder follows lightning may be knowledge, since you can very well imagine what it would be like for it to be false. But that the laws of thought should be false, or that $2+2$ should not equal 4, both of these are inconceivable. This, so far as I can see, is the main motive underlying the statement that logic and mathematics are not knowledge. And so far at any rate there is no issue. Both the naturalist and the refuter are agreed. Scientific method does not pre-suppose any other type of knowledge. For logic and mathematics are not knowledge.

The issue which we have just now discussed has turned out to be a verbal one. There are, however, related issues which are interesting. We all remember that when Socrates questioned the boy in the *Meno* he showed that the boy knew things which he had never been taught, that these things were true, and that he must have come to know them by recollection. When Kant questioned the same boy he too showed that the boy knew *a priori* things which he had never been taught, that these things were true, and that he came to know them because all little boys are like that. When today the naturalist questions that boy he discovers that boy still answering as he answered Socrates and Kant. He knows his grammar. Where did he get it? Well, grammar and the laws of thought are historical accidents. Who could have predicted that the squirrel would have such a bushy tail? Who could have predicted that a creature without any tail at all should have written the *Iliad*? You never can tell. Now Socrates was amazed at the bright boy, and describes him as a reminiscing soul on tour. He learns his mathematics in one world and is furnished with it, ready for Euclid in the next, a romance of two worlds! Kant too is puzzled by the boy, but not by the origins of his prodigy. Marvelous boy! anticipating the whole structure of the world by being the creator of it. Both Socrates and Kant did not know what we now know. The little boy is an organism, part of a long line of adaptation, missing poisons, dodging rocks, escaping tigers, milking cows, sowing seed, fetching fish, but, most important of all, saying the word. To milk a cow one must have a hand to fit and flush an udder. To say the word one must have an order to fit and flash one's prescience. What is the history of the hand, from hoof to dainty pats upon your cheek? Ask Darwin. What is the history of the laws of thought and $2+2=4$? Ask Darwin's brother. No one could have predicted what the laws of thought would be, had prediction been possible without the laws of thought.

I have no intention, however, of considering this matter further. The issue appears to be empirical. It is interesting, however, as an illustration of how the naturalist's view of scientific method, and of distinctions involved in it, is intertwined with certain results of the application of scientific method. This is the biologist's view of the origin of the *a priori*. And part of the point here is to insist that the presence of logic and mathematics are as irrelevant to the existence of anything else as is the presence of the monkey's tail. The tail like the appendix may be positively misleading. There may be a tail and no trees, and no flies. So what about the laws of thought. They too may turn out be be useless. Am I talking nonsense? I'm sorry.

And now there is a second type of refutation. The refuter goes on: "You may be quite right when you say that scientific method is successful. The libraries and the stores are full of its success. But we also know that scientific method has never been justified from a purely intellectual point of view. Now I do not necessarily mean that we know what that justification is, so that once more we have knowledge which is not arrived at by pursuing scientific method. I mean rather that this request for a justification involves a question which can not possibly be answered by any such method. If you tried to answer it in this way, your method would, of course, give rise to the same request. Hence, unless we admit that there are altogether reasonable questions, but no method at all for answering them, there must be at least one method other than scientific method for answering questions. And so it is not true that scientific method alone is successful."

And is the naturalist now quite perturbed by this? He is not. His reply might be as follows: "I think I understand you. You are assuming that a good argument must be tight like a syllogism or like a proof in geometry. That's what you mean by the phrase 'from a purely intellectual point of view.' So you are worried about the uniformity of nature, that every event in nature has a cause, that tomorrow the sun will rise, and tomorrow and tomorrow and petty-paced tomorrow. If you only knew things like this, then you would consider conclusions about fruit flies, about hydrogen, about vitamins, etc., as justified. But actually the conclusions of science are not presumed to be tight in any such sense. Now listen. It's all very simple. Yesterday and today we find uranium, under certain circumstances, behaving as though it were very angry. Tomorrow it is angry again. Next week it still behaves angrily. So we go on expecting that it will continue to do so and it does. If, however, in four weeks it should quite suddenly be mild and bleat like a little lamb, this would certainly surprise us. Who knows, however, a little angry uranium may be enough to put all the remainder fast asleep, so that even bombardment could scarcely make it yawn. Scientists after all are only human. They do no more than record the genesis of their expectations. So what we mean, in any case, by the success of scientific method is something so modest that it requires no such justification. It is justified, if you like, in the same way that your expectations generally are. If you expect to eat at six, and do eat at six, what more do you want?"

This reply is, I take it, sufficient. Refutation has failed. If you claim for science that its arguments require some necessary propositions about the order of nature, then obviously the justification of these arguments will require them. But the naturalist's account of scientific method need not involve any such necessary propositions. So once again, that scientific method is successful does not pre-suppose that there is besides this some other method.

The statement of naturalism, then, involves no contradiction. Can we not, however, move him by confronting him with a discrepant instance? No. But let's see.

Mr. Dennes says that there are no other proofs. X, which vaunteth itself a proof, comes up and says: "Am I a proof? They call me a proof." So the doctor touches a nerve, the nerve of the argument, and says: "No, you're not a proof." X replies: "But I wear a 'since' and a 'therefore.'" The doctor says: "And that's all. You've no nerve, so you're not a proof." He knows what he means by a "proof." Other candidates come up, each asking: "Am I a proof?" And the doctor separates them. Now up comes a philosophical proof. "Am I a proof?" The answer is: "No." But the proof now argues: " That's what you say, and I see what you mean, I am not the kind of proof you are talking about. My friends do not use the word 'proof' at all in the way in which you do. I'm a proof all right, but you just don't like me. So you won't call me proof. It's as though I asked you 'Am I a darling?' and you had another sweetheart, and so, of course, you said: 'No.' All the same I am a darling."

This, now, is a very difficult situation. Nobody is lying. Nobody is insincere. Does the doctor see something which the philosophical argument does not see? Maybe. He sees both types of argument, and sees that the one is good and the other is not. And what does the philosophical argument see? It sees both arguments and says that both are good. So once more if the argument asks: "And why do you say I am not a proof?" the doctor must say: "Because you are not like this." And that is all there is to it. And if this is all, then, clearly, the philosophical argument may feel thoroughly vindicated. If all the doctor means is that a philosophical argument is different from an empirical argument, the argument may respond: "Of course, that's true, but it has no bearing upon my status. After all I am another man's darling."

Suppose that he goes on to say: "No, I don't mean simply that you are not like this argument. What I mean is this: 'This type of argument is successful, and you are not.'" The response is: "And what is the criterion of success? If you mean that by means of me you can never predict the weather, well, of course, that's true. But if you ask those who love me whether I am successful, you'll get a different answer. I determine in some much subtler way the spiritual weather, and that not by prediction but by seasoning all time and eternity. Success! How would you like to be a thinking substance?"

So far as I can see there is nothing further for the doctor to do. He has judged the proof, but he can not now justify that judgment to the argument. There is no agreed-upon principle of adjudication. Further argument is futile. To each other they must continue to be queer and incomprehensible. It's as though the boys in our alley all sang out: "There's no girl but pretty Sally," and someone objected: "Oh, but that can't be!" This didn't quiet the boys. They said: "Oh, you forget that once Eve was the only girl. So it can be." And then along came Helen. "Tut! Tut!" said she, "Look at me. I'm a girl," to which the boys responded, "No, you're not." And when she said "Prove it," they laughed, told her to go home and be quiet. "You're just a girl out of a store window, that's what you are."

So far I have shown that you can not refute this apparent main thesis of naturalism. You can not do it by detecting any contradiction, nor by adducing any evidence. And you can not do this because there is no thesis. When Mr. Krikorian speaks of this sentence as a basic belief, this is strictly a mistake. There is no belief at all. There is no belief because nothing has been said which could be false.

How, then, are these several sentences to be interpreted? I think that something like this may do. These sentences are strictly an enunciation of policy. In effect they say: "Let us be scientific." And negatively: "No more metaphysics." In a sober and quiet way a naturalist might say: "I've tried to do metaphysics. I can't grasp it. So I've turned to matters within my reach and grasp. I can do botany so much better. Or I can cut hair or polish teeth." If this were now what naturalists did, there would, I think, be no mystery at all. What causes the difficulty is that having said: "We are going to do science," they do not do science. If a man who sold groceries suddenly tired of selling groceries, exclaimed: "Enough! I am going to wash automobiles," and went out and washed automobiles, there would be no puzzle about this. But if he repeated his resolution frequently, put on his hat and coat and walked to the door, and then started for the other side of the store to sort potatoes, what then? Well, so it is.

Is, then, naturalism, in any case, a good policy? I think that the naturalists' defense is this. Metaphysics and science aim at the same thing. Metaphysics fails. Science succeeds. Accordingly, naturalism is nothing but adoption of the successful policy. Who, to get home, would deliberately take the way that won't get him there? And the naturalist might go on. Even though it were true that metaphysics and science do not aim at the same thing, it is clear that metaphysics fails in whatever it aims at, whereas science succeeds. How foolish, then, to engage in failure. So in either case naturalism is the best policy.

Once more, then, the dispute breaks out. Do metaphysics and science aim at the same thing? Is metaphysics a failure? Disregarding, for the moment, the obscurity of both these questions, I should, throwing my words about wildly, make this noise. Metaphysics and science do not aim at the same thing. And now I should first like to explain this. Metaphysics arises out of the fact that men come to have a variety of beliefs,

beliefs about God, about how they should live, about the material world, about their own other-worldly destiny, etc. Some expurgated people escape nearly all such beliefs, but most people either believe or are uneasy. In any case, with respect to such beliefs, men have tried to do two things. They have first tried to prove that what they believe is true. In this respect there certainly is an analogy between science and metaphysics, and this may be what justifies the naturalist thesis. For if he now also holds that it is precisely in this respect that metaphysics has failed, namely, in its attempt to prove, then I, at least, am inclined to agree that he is right. For there is in metaphysics no criterion of proof. I take it that there is among metaphysicians no agreement upon even one purported proof. If, then, the purpose of metaphysics is to prove, metaphysics provides no intelligible account of what this could be.

This is not, however, the whole story. Men have also tried in their metaphysical adventures to weave together the contents of their beliefs into some coherent pattern, to keep more steadfastly before their minds the scene of their hopes, their aspirations, and their fears. In the past the aim to prove has clouded and vexed this endeavor by an ungainly and tortured vocabulary, but, even so, the present ruins in some way, no doubt, served. I expect that varieties of belief will continue, and that this motive to elaborate and to fashion a crazy or a sane quilt in which to wrap oneself against all temporary weathers will continue. And I do not mind. I shall continue to be entertained by it, and will in one instance even love it. Nevertheless, I think that metaphysics with this single aim will, when successful, be much more like poetry or a novel than like the metaphysics which, with divided and obscure aims, has puzzled and pleased men in the past.

Naturalism, as a policy, is then no mystery. It has seized upon a certain clear notion of proof, and in the light of this clear notion of proof it is easy to see from what defect metaphysics has come to be so sick. Metaphysics will walk again only when it surrenders pretension to proof, and, as humbly as the Apostles' Creed, begins its words with: I believe!

DESCARTES' EVIL GENIUS

THERE WAS ONCE AN EVIL GENIUS who promised the mother of us all that if she ate of the fruit of the tree, she would be like God, knowing good and evil. He promised knowledge. She did eat and she learned, but she was disappointed, for to know good and evil and not to be God is awful. Many an Eve later, there was rumor of another evil genius. This evil genius promised no good, promised no knowledge. He made a boast, a boast so wild and so deep and so dark that those who heard it cringed in hearing it. And what was that boast? Well, that apart from a few, four or five, clear and distinct ideas, he could deceive any son of Adam about anything. So he boasted. And with some result? Some indeed! Men going about in the brightest noonday would look and exclaim: "How obscure!" and if some careless merchant counting his apples was heard to say: "Two and three are five," a hearer of the boast would rub his eyes and run away. This evil genius still whispers, thundering, among the leaves of books, frightening people, whispering: "I can. Maybe I will. Maybe so, maybe not." The tantalizer! In what follows I should like to examine the boast of this evil genius.

I am referring, of course, to that evil genius of whom Descartes writes:

> I shall then suppose, not that God who is supremely good and the fountain of truth, but some evil genius not less

powerful than deceitful, has employed his whole energies in deceiving me; I shall consider that the heavens, the earth, the colors, figures, sound, and all other external things are nought but illusions and dreams of which this evil genius has availed himself, in order to lay traps for my credulity; I shall consider myself as having no hands, no eyes, no flesh, no blood, nor any senses, yet falsely believing myself to possess all these things.[1]

This then is the evil genius whom I have represented as boasting that he can deceive us about all these things. I intend now to examine this boast, and to understand how this deceiving and being deceived are to take place. I expect to discover that the evil genius may very well deceive us, but that if we are wary, we need not be deceived. He will deceive us, if he does, by bathing the word "illusion" in a fog. This then will be the word to keep our minds on. In order to accomplish all this, I intend to describe the evil genius carrying out his boast in two adventures. The first of these I shall consider a thoroughly transparent case of deception. The word "illusion" will find a clear and familiar application. Nevertheless in this instance the evil genius will not have exhausted "his whole energies in deceiving us." Hence we must aim to imagine a further trial of the boast, in which the "whole energies" of the evil genius are exhausted. In this instance I intend to show that the evil genius is himself befuddled, and that if we too exhaust some of our energies in sleuthing after the peculiarities in his diction, then we need not be deceived either.

Let us imagine the evil genius then at his ease meditating that very bad is good enough for him, and that he would let bad enough alone. All the old pseudos, pseudo names and pseudo statements, are doing very well. But today it was different. He took no delight in common lies, everyday fibs, little ones, old

[1] *Philosophical Works of Descartes*, trans. E. S. Haldane and G. R. T. Ross (2 vols.; Cambridge: Cambridge University Press, 1912), I, 147.

ones. He wanted something new and something big. He scratched his genius; he uncovered an idea. And he scribbled on the inside of his tattered halo, " Tomorrow, I will deceive," and he smiled, and his words were thin and like fine wire. "Tomorrow I will change everything, everything, everything. I will change flowers, human beings, trees, hills, sky, the sun, and everything else into paper. Paper alone I will not change. There will be paper flowers, paper human beings, paper trees. And human beings will be deceived. They will think that there are flowers, human beings, and trees, and there will be nothing but paper. It will be gigantic. And it ought to work. After all men have been deceived with much less trouble. There was a sailor, a Baptist I believe, who said that all was water. And there was no more water then than there is now. And there was a pool-hall keeper who said that all was billiard balls. That's a long time ago of course, a long time before they opened one, and listening, heard that it was full of the sound of a trumpet. My prospects are good. I'll try it."

And the evil genius followed his own directions and did according to his words. And this is what happened.

Imagine a young man, Tom, bright today as he was yesterday, approaching a table where yesterday he had seen a bowl of flowers. Today it suddenly strikes him that they are not flowers. He stares at them troubled, looks away, and looks again. Are they flowers? He shakes his head. He chuckles to himself. "Huh! that's funny. Is this a trick? Yesterday there certainly were flowers in that bowl." He sniffs suspiciously, hopefully, but smells nothing. His nose gives no assurance. He thinks of the birds that flew down to peck at the grapes in the picture and of the mare that whinnied at the likeness of Alexander's horse. Illusions! The picture oozed no juice, and the likeness was still. He walked slowly to the bowl of flowers. He looked, and he sniffed, and he raised his hand. He stroked a petal lightly, lover of flowers, and he drew back. He could scarcely believe his fingers. They were not flowers. They were paper.

As he stands, perplexed, Milly, friend and dear, enters the

room. Seeing him occupied with the flowers, she is about to take up the bowl and offer them to him, when once again he is overcome with feelings of strangeness. She looks just like a great big doll. He looks more closely, closely as he dares, seeing this may be Milly after all. Milly, are you Milly ?—that wouldn't do. Her mouth clicks as she opens it, speaking, and it shuts precisely. Her forehead shines, and he shudders at the thought of Mme Tussaud's. Her hair is plaited, evenly, perfectly, like Milly's but as she raises one hand to guard its order, touching it, preening, it whispers like a newspaper. Her teeth are white as a genteel monthly. Her gums are pink, and there is a clapper in her mouth. He thinks of mama dolls, and of the rubber doll he used to pinch; it had a misplaced navel right in the pit of the back, that whistled. Galatea in paper! Illusions!

He noted all these details, flash by flash by flash. He reaches for a chair to steady himself and just in time. She approaches with the bowl of flowers, and, as the bowl is extended towards him, her arms jerk. The suppleness, the smoothness, the roundness of life is gone. Twitches of a smile mislight up her face. He extends his hand to take up the bowl and his own arms jerk as hers did before. He takes the bowl, and as he does so sees his hand. It is pale, fresh, snowy. Trembling, he drops the bowl, but it does not break, and the water does not run. What a mockery!

He rushes to the window, hoping to see the real world. The scene is like a theatre-set. Even the pane in the window is drawn very thin, like cellophane. In the distance are the forms of men walking about and tossing trees and houses and boulders and hills upon the thin cross section of a truck that echoes only echoes of chugs as it moves. He looks into the sky upward, and it is low. There is a patch straight above him, and one seam is loose. The sun shines out of the blue like a drop of German silver. He reaches out with his pale hand, crackling the cellophane, and his hand touches the sky. The sky shakes and tiny bits of it fall, flaking his white hand with confetti.

Make-believe!

He retreats, crinkling, creaking, hiding his sight. As he moves he misquotes a line of poetry: "Those are perils that were his eyes," and he mutters, "Hypocritical pulp!" He goes on: "I see that the heavens, the earth, colors, figures, sound, and all other external things, flowers, Milly, trees and rocks and hills are paper, paper laid as traps for my credulity. Paper flowers, paper Milly, paper sky!" Then he paused, and in sudden fright he asked "And what about me?" He reaches to his lip and with two fingers tears the skin and peels off a strip of newsprint. He looks at it closely, grim. "I shall consider myself as having no hands, no eyes, no flesh, no blood, or any senses." He lids his paper eyes and stands dejected. Suddenly he is cheered. He exclaims: "*Cogito me papyrum esse, ergo sum.*" He has triumphed over paperdom.

I have indulged in this phantasy in order to illustrate the sort of situation which Descartes' words might be expected to describe. The evil genius attempts to deceive. He tries to mislead Tom into thinking what is not. Tom is to think that these are flowers, that this is the Milly that was, that those are trees, hills, the heavens, etc. And he does this by creating illusions, that is, by making something that looks like flowers, artificial flowers; by making something that looks like and sounds like and moves like Milly, an artificial Milly. An illusion is something that looks like or sounds like, so much like, something else that you either mistake it for something else, or you can easily understand how someone might come to do this. So when the evil genius creates illusions intending to deceive he makes things which might quite easily be mistaken for what they are not. Now in the phantasy as I discovered it Tom is not deceived. He does experience the illusion, however. The intention of this is not to cast any reflection upon the deceptive powers of the evil genius. With such refinements in the paper art as we now know, the evil genius might very well have been less unsuccessful. And that in spite of his rumored lament: "And I made her of the best paper!" No, that Tom is not deceived, that he detects the illusion, is introduced in order to remind ourselves how illusions are detected. That the paper flowers are illusory is revealed by the recognition that they are paper. As soon as Tom realizes that though they look like flowers but are paper, he is acquainted with, sees through the illusion, and is not deceived. What is required, of course, is that he know the difference between flowers and paper, and that when presented with one or the other he can tell the difference. The attempt of the evil genius also presupposes this. What he intends is that though Tom knows this difference, the paper will look so much like flowers that Tom will not notice the respect in which the paper is different from the flowers. And even though Tom had actually been deceived and had not recognized the illusion, the evil genius himself must have been aware of the difference, for this is involved in his design. This is crucial, as we shall see when we come to consider the second adventure of the evil genius.

As you will remember I have represented the foregoing as an illustration of the sort of situation which Descartes' words might be expected to describe. Now, however, I think that this is misleading. For though I have described a situation in which there are many things, nearly all of which are calculated to serve as illusions, this question may still arise. Would this paper world still be properly described as a world of illusions? If Tom says: "These are flowers," or "These look like flowers" (uncertainly), then the illusion is operative. But if Tom says: "These are paper," then the illusion has been destroyed. Descartes uses the words: "And all other external things are nought but illusions." This means that the situation which Descartes has in mind is such that if Tom says: "These are flowers," he will be wrong, but he will be wrong also if he says: "These are paper," and it won't matter what sentence of that type he uses. If he says: "These are rock"—or cotton or cloud or wood—he is wrong by the plan. He will be right only if he says: "These are illusions." But the project is to keep him from recognizing the illusions. This means that the illusions are to be brought about not by anything so crude as paper or even cloud. They must be made of the stuff that dreams are made of.

Now let us consider this second adventure.

The design then is this. The evil genius is to create a world of illusions. There are to be no flowers, no Milly, no paper. There is to be nothing at all, but Tom is every moment to go on mistaking nothing for something, nothing at all for flowers, nothing at all for Milly, etc. This is, of course, quite different from mistaking paper for flowers, paper for Milly. And yet all is to be arranged in such a way that Tom will go on just as we now do, and just as Tom did before the paper age, to see, hear, smell the world. He will love the flowers, he will kiss Milly, he will blink at the sun. So he thinks. And in thinking about these things he will talk and argue just as we do. But all the time he will be mistaken. There are no flowers, there is no kiss, there is no sun. Illusions all. This then is the end at which the evil genius aims.

How now is the evil genius to attain this end? Well, it is clear that a part of what he aims at will be realized if he destroys everything. Then there will be no flowers, and if Tom thinks that there are flowers he will be wrong. There will be no face that is Milly's and no tumbled beauty on her head, and if Tom thinks that there is Milly's face and Milly's hair, he will be wrong. It is necessary then to see to it that there are none of these things. So the evil genius, having failed with paper, destroys even all paper. Now there is nothing to see, nothing to hear, nothing to smell, etc. But this is not enough to deceive. For though Tom sees nothing, and neither hears nor smells anything, he may also think that he sees nothing. He must also be misled into thinking that he does see something, that there are flowers and Milly, and hands, eyes, flesh, blood, and all other senses. Accordingly the evil genius restores to Tom his old life. Even the memory of that paper day is blotted out, not a scrap remains. Witless Tom lives on, thinking, hoping, loving as he used to, unwitted by the great destroyer. All that seems so solid, so touchable to seeming hands, so biteable to apparent teeth, is so flimsy that were the evil genius to poke his index at it, it would curl away save for one tiny trace, the smirch of that index. So once more the evil genius has done according to his word.

And now let us examine the result.

I should like first of all to describe a passage of Tom's life. Tom is all alone, but he doesn't know it. What an opportunity for methodologico-metaphysico-solipsimo! I intend, in any case, to disregard the niceties of his being so alone and to borrow his own words, with the warning that the evil genius smiles as he reads them. Tom writes:

> Today, as usual, I came into the room and there was the bowl of flowers on the table. I went up to them, caressed them, and smelled over them. I thank God for flowers! There's nothing so real to me as flowers. Here the genuine essence of the world's substance, at its gayest and most hilarious speaks to me. It seems unworthy even to think of them as erect, and waving on pillars of sap. Sap! Sap!

There was more in the same vein, which we need not bother to record. I might say that the evil genius was a bit amused, snickered in fact, as he read the words "so real," "essence," "substance," etc., but later he frowned and seemed puzzled. Tom went on to describe how Milly came into the room, and how glad he was to see her. They talked about the flowers. Later he walked to the window and watched the gardener clearing a space a short distance away. The sun was shining, but there were a few heavy clouds. He raised the window, extended his hand and four large drops of rain wetted his hand. He returned to the room and quoted to Milly a song from *The Tempest*. He got all the words right, and was well pleased with himself. There was more he wrote, but this was enough to show how quite normal everything seems. And, too, how successful the evil genius is.

And the evil genius said to himself, not quite in solipsimo, "Not so, not so, not at all so."

The evil genius was, however, all too human. Admiring himself but unadmired, he yearned for admiration. To deceive but to be unsuspected is too little glory. The evil genius set about then to plant the seeds of suspicion. But how to do this? Clearly there was no suggestive paper to tempt Tom's confidence. There was nothing but Tom's mind, a stream of seemings and of words to make the seemings seem no seemings. The evil genius must have words with Tom and must engage the same seemings with him. To have words with Tom is to have the words together, to use them in the same way, and to engage the same seemings is to see and to hear and to point to the same. And so the evil genius, free spirit, entered in at the door of Tom's pineal gland and lodged there. He floated in the humors that flow, glandwise and sensewise, everywhere being as much one with Tom as difference will allow. He looked out of the same eyes, and when Tom pointed with his finger, the evil genius said "This" and meant what Tom, hearing, also meant, seeing. Each heard with the same ear what the other heard. For every sniffing of the one nose there were two identical smells, and there were two tactualities for every touch. If Tom had had a toothache, together they would have pulled the same face. The twinsomeness of two monads finds here the limit of identity. Nevertheless there was otherness looking out of those eyes as we shall see.

It seems then that on the next day, the evil genius "going to and fro" in Tom's mind and "walking up and down in it," Tom once again, as his custom was, entered the room where the flowers stood on the table. He stopped, looked admiringly, and in a caressing voice said: "Flowers! Flowers!" And he lingered. The evil genius, more subtle "than all the beasts of the field," whispered "Flowers? Flowers?" For the first time Tom has an intimation of company, of some intimate partner in perception. Momentarily he is checked. He looks again at the flowers. "Flowers? Why, of course, flowers." Together they look out of the same eyes. Again the evil genius whispers, "Flowers?" The seed of suspicion is to be the question. But Tom now raises the flowers nearer to his eyes almost violently as though his eyes were not his own. He is, however, not perturbed. The evil

genius only shakes their head. "Did you ever hear of illusions?"
says he.

Tom, still surprisingly good-natured, responds: "But you
saw them, didn't you? Surely you can see through my eyes. Come,
let us bury my nose deep in these blossoms, and take one long
breath together. Then tell whether you can recognize these as
flowers."

So they dunked the one nose. But the evil genius said "Huh!"
as much as to say: What has all this seeming and smelling to do
with it? Still he explained nothing. And Tom remained as
confident of the flowers as he had been at the first. The little
seeds of doubt, "Flowers? Flowers?" and again "Flowers?"
and "Illusions?" and now this stick in the spokes, "Huh!"
made Tom uneasy. He went on: "Oh, so you are one of these
seers that has to touch everything. You're a tangibilite. Very
well, here's my hand, let's finger these flowers. Careful! They're
tender."

The evil genius was amused. He smiled inwardly and rippled
in a shallow humor. To be taken for a materialist! As though the
grand illusionist was not a spirit! Nevertheless, he realized that
though deception is easy where the lies are big enough (where
had he heard that before?), a few scattered, questioning words
are not enough to make guile grow. He was tempted to make a
statement, and he did. He said, "Your flowers are nothing but
illusions."

"My flowers illusions?" exclaimed Tom, and he took up the
bowl and placed it before a mirror. "See," said he, "here are the
flowers and here, in the mirror, is an illusion. There's a difference
surely. And you with my eyes, my nose, and my fingers can tell
what that difference is. Pollen on your fingers touching the
illusion? send Milly the flowers in the mirror? Set a bee to
suck honey out of this glass? You know all this as well as I do.
I can tell flowers from illusions, and my flowers, as you now
plainly see, are not illusions."

The evil genius was now sorely tried. He had his make-
believe, but he also had his pride. Would he now risk the make-
believe to save his pride? Would he explain? He explained.

"Tom," he said, "notice. The flowers in the mirror look like flowers, but they only look like flowers. We agree about that. The flowers before the mirror also look like flowers. But they, you say, are flowers because they also smell like flowers and they feel like flowers, as though they would be any more flowers because they also like flowers multiply. Imagine a mirror such that it reflected not only the looks of flowers, but also their fragance and their petal surfaces, and then you smelled and touched, and the flowers before the mirror would be just like the flowers in the mirror. Then you could see immediately that the flowers before the mirror are illusions just as those in the mirror are illusions. As it is now, it is clear that the flowers in the mirror are thin illusions, and the flowers before the mirror are thick. Thick illusions are the best for deception. And they may be as thick as you like. From them you may gather pollen, send them to Milly, and foolish bees may sleep in them."

But Tom was not asleep. "I see that what you mean by thin illusions is what I mean by illusions, and what you mean by thick illusions is what I mean by flowers. So when you say that my flowers are your thick illusions this doesn't bother me. And as for your mirror that mirrors all layers of your thick illusions, I shouldn't call that a mirror at all. It's a duplicator, and much more useful than a mirror, provided you can control it. But I do suppose that when you speak of thick illusions you do mean that thick illusions are related to something you call flowers in much the same way that the thin illusions are related to the thick ones. Is that true?"

The evil genius was now diction-deep in explanations and went on. "In the first place let me assure you that these are not flowers. I destroyed all flowers. There are no flowers at all. There are only thin and thick illusions of flowers. I can see your flowers in the mirror, and I can smell and touch the flowers before the mirror. What I cannot smell and touch, having seen as in the mirror, is not even thick illusion. But if I cannot also *cerpicio* what I see, smell, touch, etc., what I have then seen is not anything real. *Esse est cerpici.* I just now tried to *cerpicio* your flowers, but there was nothing there. Man is after all a four- or five- or six-sense creature and you cannot expect much from so little."

Tom rubbed his eyes and his ears tingled with an eighteenth-century disturbance. Then he stared at the flowers. "I see," he said, "that this added sense of yours has done wickedly with our language. You do not mean by illusion what we mean, and neither do you mean by flowers what we mean. As for *cerpicio* I wouldn't be surprised if you'd made up that word just to puzzzle us. In any case what you destroyed is what, according to you, you used to *cerpicio*. So there is nothing for you to *cerpicio* any more. But there still are what we mean by flowers. If your intention was to deceive, you must learn the language of those you are to deceive. I should say that you are like the doctor who prescribes for his patients what is so bad for himself and is then surprised at the health of his patients." And he pinned a flower near their nose.

The evil genius, discomfited, rode off on a corpuscle. He had failed. He took to an artery, made haste to the pineal exit, and was gone. Then "sun by sun" he fell. And he regretted his mischief.

I have tried in this essay to understand the boast of the evil genius. His boast was that he could deceive, deceive about "the heavens, the earth, the colors, figures, sound, and all other external things." In order to do this I have tried to bring clearly to mind what deception and such deceiving would be like. Such deception involves illusions and such deceiving involves the creation of illusions. Accordingly I have tried to imagine the evil genius engaged in the practice of deception, busy in the creation of illusions. In the first adventure everything is plain. The evil genius employs paper, paper making believe it's many other things. The effort to deceive, ingenuity in deception, being deceived by paper, detecting the illusion—all these are clearly understood. It is the second adventure, however, which is more crucial. For in this instance it is assumed that the illusion is of such a kind that no seeing, no touching, no smelling, are relevant to detecting the illusion. Nevertheless the evil genius sees, touches, smells, and does detect the illusion. He made the illusion; so, of course, he must know it. How then does he know it? The evil genius has a sense denied to men. He senses the flower-in-itself, Milly-in-her-self, etc. So he creates illusions made up of what can be seen, heard, smelled, etc., illusions all because when seeing, hearing, and smelling have seen, heard, and smelled all, the special sense senses nothing. So what poor human beings sense is the illusion of what only the evil genius can sense. This is formidable. Nevertheless, once again everything is clear. If we admit the special sense, then we can readily see how it is that the evil genius should have been so confident. He has certainly created his own illusions, though he has not himself been deceived. But neither has anyone else been deceived. For human beings do not use the word " illusion" by relation to a sense with which only the evil genius is blessed.

I said that the evil genius had not been deceived, and it is true that he has not been deceived by his own illusions. Nevertheless he was deceived in boasting that he could deceive, for his confidence in this is based upon an ignorance of the difference between our uses of the words, "heavens," "earth," " flowers," "Milly," and "illusions" of these things, and his own uses of these words. For though there certainly is an analogy between our own uses and his, the difference is quite sufficient to explain his failure at grand deception. We can also understand how easily Tom might have been taken in. The dog over the water dropped his meaty bone for a picture on the water. Tom, however, dropped nothing at all. But the word "illusion" is a trap.

I began this essay uneasily, looking at my hands and saying "no hands," blinking my eyes and saying "no eyes." Everything I saw seemed to me like something Cheshire, a piece of cheese, for instance, appearing and disappearing in the leaves of the tree. Poor kitty! And now? Well....

THE MYSTERY OF TIME
(OR, THE MAN WHO DID NOT
KNOW WHAT TIME IS)

THE OCCASION OF THIS ESSAY is the remark of a student, which he made after a company of us had tried to assure him that if he knew how to answer such questions as: What time is it? and when were you born? and are you going soon? and were you always lazy? etc., then he would also know what time is. He protested, however, that though he certainly did know all these things, he still did not know what time is. Accordingly I want to study two cases of men who do not know what time is. The first is to be one which is exceedingly simple and which I want to use in order to exhibit a clear case of not knowing what time is. The second is a case which I have found baffling, and which is authentic. I think that I have succeeded in discovering in this case just what it is that the man who does not know what time is, does not know. In a middle part of this essay I have reviewed a small part of the language of time in order to show how rich this is in ramifications, which then one may, according to one's disposition, play in, as children do in a large and empty house, or which then one may lose oneself in, as older people also do. What, in certain aspects, makes this a playground is what also makes it a labyrinth.

I

Once upon a space there was a man who laid linoleum, a fantastical fellow, who did not believe in clocks. He would get up from the floor, his measuring foot in hand, and stare at the clock, laying down his measure in this direction and that, round about the clock. Sometimes he would move his hand through the air in the neighborhood of the clock as though he were trying to feel something, a current or stream. "Nothing there," he would mutter as he returned to his linoleum on the floor, patting the linoleum, pleased to rest his hand on something tangible. He'd go on taking measurements and at intervals he would caress his measuring stick and would talk to it. A few minutes later he would look up at the clock, almost angrily. The clock went on ticking. At times he'd clench his fist. Whole mornings he would pass in this way, making love to his foot-rule and fighting the clock. He would speak scornfully of everything pertaining to the clock, calling it an imposter. "Time," he would say, "time, seconds, minutes, hours, days, knights and their ladies. Bah!" He was grim. Then he'd look at his ruler. "Tell me, tell me, how many inches in an hour?" And he'd look at the clock and come down hard on the next nail in the linoleum.

There have, of course, been other strange encounters with clocks and watches. In the inventory which the Lilliputians made of what they found in the pockets of Gulliver is the following note: "Out of the right fob hung a great silver chain, with a wonderful kind of engine at the bottom. We directed him to draw out whatever was fastened to that chain; which appeared to be a globe, half silver, and half some transparent metal: for on the transparent side we saw certain strange figures circularly drawn, and thought we could touch them, till we found our fingers stopped by that lucid substance. He put this engine to our ears, which made an incessant noise like that of a watermill, and we conjecture it is either some unknown animal, or the god that he worships; but we are more inclined to the latter opinion, because he assures us (if we understood him right, for he expressed himself very imperfectly) that he seldom does anything without consulting it: he called it his oracle, and said it pointed out the time for every action of his life." Later the Emperor "was amazed at the continual noise it made, and the motion of the minute hand, which he could easily discern; for their sight is much more acute than ours; and asked the opinions of his learned men about him, which were various and remote, as the reader may well imagine without my repeating; although indeed I could not very perfectly understand them." But my only point now is to point out that the man who laid linoleum is not the first to have been mystified by a watch or clock. Besides I'm not through telling about him.

Of course, this man was not simply curious. He was quite disturbed. It was no joke. All his life he had been familiar with clocks. They had had ever so many times together until this "antic disposition" took hold of him. And so it was on the day of which I was speaking. In the evening he visited his friend the clockmaker, seated in the midst of his clock-works, taking tictation and tightening short-hands. He entered the clock-shop, glanced hurriedly about with both ears, and sat down. Not much was said at first. This was a clock-shop and two hundred clocks stared down at him. Pendulumonium! At eight o'clock the whole clock-works began to move, bells rang out from tiny clock-steeples, roosters crowed on tiny perches, cuckoos clock-cooed from tiny balconies, and eight assorted insects flew past a waiting bird as she gobbled up the hours. On the face of one trick clock, the minute hand was extended from the face of the clock, its fingers outspread with the end of the thumb resting on the tip of what seemed to be a nose raised in the center. Fortunately he did not see this. But he did see and hear too much. He could bear it no longer. Most absurd thing! "Ach," he cried, getting up from his chair, "Your clocks! Your clocks! What do they mean, your clocks?" and he gave a short kick in the direction of the case set in order with clocks before him. The clocks went on ticking, tick, tick, not heeding.

"Come," he said, with marvelous self-control, "I see your

clocks. Now show me time, not ages, not aeons, but just one minute, and then I'll believe in your clocks." And he handed him his foot-rule. The clock-maker smiled, embarrassed, and glanced at his clocks. Plainly he felt responsible, but he returned the foot-rule. "I'm in earnest," his friend continued. "Today I fought your clock. I threw my hammer at it. And missed. Look!" And he got down on his hands and knees and measured the long side of the linoleum in the clock-maker's shop. "There," he said. "I measured the linoleum. Here's my foot-rule. You saw how I laid it down, laid it down, again and again, and counted to twelve. There are twelve feet on this side. You see the linoleum and you see the foot-rule. Now, then, as I have just shown you, so now you show me twelve minutes of time. Twelve feet of linoleum, twelve minutes of time! If, for instance, you got down on your knees with the clock in your hand and measured the linoleum, and counted thirty-six minutes of linoleum, then, I should understand how you were using the clock and what you were measuring. Or if you rolled your clock from one edge of the linoleum to the other, and you counted the rolls, that too would suit me. There might be circular foot-rules. But how do you manage to get down on your hands and knees or whatever you do, and so hold time down flat, and pull it straight so that you can get your measurement? Linoleum, five minutes flat."

He was in dead earnest. The clock-maker rubbed the bristles on his chin and tried not to be afraid. He looked about him and looked into the faces of his clocks. There was no help there. In his desperation he picked up a clock and was about to get down on his knees with the clock in his measuring hand, when another of his clocks rang off and a cuckoo stepped out and cocked its little head in his direction. The clock-maker, crouched as he was on one knee, looked up and burst out laughing. He set the clock back on the shelf. The layer of linoleum did not smile. He looked grimly at the cuckoo still cocking its head and the whole hickory-dickory-dock shebang. Dumb clocks! And he thought of that man who had made the largest machine in the world, which could do nothing, which also could not measure linoleum. He frowned and he got the notion that clocks were designed to make fun of laying linoleum, as though laying linoleum consisted of nothing but raising two hands and counting up to twelve. He was getting angry. " Listen," said the clock-maker, "the clock isn't used in that way and time isn't like an edge of the linoleum. There are other forms of measure. You can't pour linoleum into a cup nor squeeze it out of an eye-dropper. Ten drops of linoleum! Trying to explain to someone what a twelve-foot length of linoleum is like, by showing him how an eye-dropper works—well, that won't do any good. You don't talk about pounds, ounces, and pence in giving a man change for a kilo-cycle. There are all sorts of measures." He paused. Then he brightened. "Did you ever read this line in Black: 'Can wisdom be put in a silver-rod or love in a golden-bowl?' You just try it." He felt that he was doing pretty well. He was rising in his own estimation and began to feel airy. "And here is a line from such another: 'I have measured out my life in coffee-spoons.'" Then he switched. "Ah," he said. "I think I can explain clocks to you. Do you know the hour-glass and the sun dial?" But it was too late. His friend was not listening. Ever since the idea of pouring linoleum and the idea of the eye-dropper had been mentioned, he was pre-occupied. He was talking to himself, asking: What is time? and pausing, and then going on: What is water? He was trying to get the hang of his own question and when he thought of water he felt much better. If only he could meet time, as he could meet water, dipping his delighting fingers into it, then he might yet be a friend of clocks. He got up, musing, waved his hand to the clock-maker, and then, looking about him, he waved to the clock too. "Good," he said, "If I can manage to figure time in liters, I'll shake hands with all of you," and he made a gesture as though he were about to shake hands with a clock. They all ticked back at him, speeding up their tempo, and fidgeting with their hands. At least so it seemed to him. "Keep quiet," he shouted, and a chorus of clocks shouted back to him: "We keep time." He rushed out.

He walked. As he passed the town-hall, he looked up at the great wheel in the tower. It began striking the hour and boomed down at him. He winced at every stroke, covered his ears, and walked faster. He hurried on to his friend, an expert in water-meters. His friend saw him coming. "Good!" he said to himself. "We'll play a game of bridge," an excellent game, by the way, for people so much occupied with water. They greeted each other, but it was soon evident that there was to be no game of bridge. His visitor began at once: "Listen, listen," he cried. "Will you show me the workings of your water-meter?" He gave no explanation and his friend asked no question. "Well," he said, and he showed him a model meter incased in glass, all its secrets open, its outsides transparent. His visitor studied it carefully, saw where the water runs into the water-meter and out again, and he read the chasing figures, 1, 2, 3, 4,..., and he saw that all was wet as it should be. It ticked like a clock and this especially pleased him. "Ah," he said, "I'm on the right track. I see the water and I see the measure-chamber, gulping and spilling measures of water, as the water flows. And there are the numbers." Satisfaction warmed his face. "Wonderful! Wonderful! Forty gallons, so many cubic feet of water, have run through the chamber while I watched the numbers goose-trot through the opening. Water plain as linoleum!" He felt thoroughly relaxed. This is what he wanted to see. Now for the clock. "If only I had a transparent clock, then I should see time flow as now I saw the water in this meter flow. Time meter! Time flows. Time like a river. "'Time, like an everflowing stream.'" The more he saw and the more he said, the more he felt assured.

The water-meter master watched his friend curiously, but understood neither his excitement nor his words. He realized that there was some concern about a clock and about time, and he glanced at the old grandfather pendu-slumbering in the corner. Nothing striking about that! He was glad in any case that his water-meter had been useful. "What's the matter?" he asked. "Has your clock stopped?" His friend looked at him

troubled. "Clock stopped? Clock stopped? Was it going somewhere?" And he looked serious. "No, indeed. My foot-rule is
clogged. Can't tell time on your water-meter." He sniffed.
Obviously he was not going to explain. The other shook his
head, slipped a cover over the water-meter, and drew out his
watch. He handed it over to his friend, who looked at it, turning
it over carefully, then he glanced in the direction of the water-
meter. Then he returned it without a word. A minute or two
later he said: "I must be going." And he left.

So the friend of linoleum went home. He walked up the stairs,
trying to make a noise like a clock, ticking, just to work up his
sympathies, hoping in this way to understand the clock. When
he got to his room, he walked straight to the clock and sat down
on the bed to examine it. He turned it upside down, and turned
it round and round. He shook it and he squeezed it. He noticed
the knobs and keys on the back-side of it. He was taking time
seriously, almost anxiously. He looked for an opening to discover where time comes in and he found one at the top just
under the bell, and he held his hand over it, but the clock went
on ticking and he felt no time on his hand. He shook the clock
again, hoping to catch a few seconds seeping through the seams
from the inside, but he saw only a fine spray of dust sifting down
on the table. He was, however, in no mood to take time for that
or that for time—though he was at first startled to see it, was for
a moment hopeful. "Ah!" he exclaimed. But then he knew.
Finally he decided to take the clock apart, to get a look inside.
"Clocks keep time. Well, we'll see." And so, poor fellow, he
undid the clock. He was not a bit surprised. The insides of the
clock were not even wet. There was not a sparkle of temporal
dew even in the spring. He sighed. He gathered the debris of his
clock in his hands and laid it on a chair. And he could not
imagine how time, had there really been some, could have
escaped him. He had been so careful.

But this was not the end of his perplexity. He went on trying
to puzzle out how the clock could be measuring something. In
his most meticulous fashion he would say: "Well, perhaps the

clock does measure something. Per hand from six to twelve is six units of the push of the turn of the index-thumb against the key that winds the spring that unwinds against the cog that moves with the wheel that goes tick." And then he would write this down and snuggle up to it, it was so reasonable. "So one o'clock is so much of the push of the index-thumb against the key spent in the progress of the hand from some point in the circumference of the face to another point in the circumference of the same face, semi-ambi-dextrous to the center." And so too the hour-glass measures sand. On other days he would review what he had said before. "Is push time? But why, then, does a man, when he looks at his watch, run for a bus?" And he would hold his head. And then he would come up with another theory. "Time," he would say, "is invisible, an invisible water, and it flows through clocks and is gulped and spilled in upsy-downsy containers, ticken upwards and ticken downwards, as the invisible flows," And this is right too, for is not time invisible? What a comfort in comparison with time linoleum is, so simple— and visible, too! And water, too. But his speculation was not always so gentle. There were times when he suspected clock-makers of a grand conspiracy, obviously, for profit, imposing their machines upon all the people and teaching them a language to go with it, and calling their watches and clocks time-pieces. And the people had now been taken in for some generations, so that though people knew very well what the insides of a clock are like, one seldom heard of anyone doing as he had done, investigating a clock to find out whether there was anything in it. "Time is an illusion, a mere appearance," he would say, "engineered by people who are giving us the works." He thought it un-American too.

II

In the preceding section, I have, as I indicated earlier, presented the simple case of a man who does not know what time is. It is obvious enough that he approaches the clock with the foot-rule, expecting to discover something vaguely like linoleum, and that later he approaches it with the expectation that it, the clock, works like a water-meter, and that something vaguely like water runs through the clock. Knowing what time is would in this case be something like feeling the drift of time against the surface or against the edge of one's foot-rule or like feeling something soft as a baby's breath in the palm of one's hand as one shakes the clock over it. Time tipping the edge of a foot-rule, time on one's hands! The explanation is, I think, also obvious. This man knows to begin with that we measure linoleum, water, and time. How much linoleum? How much water? How much time? He also knows how to measure linoleum, and discovers how to measure water. He understands the use of the foot-rule and also the use of the water-meter. Now, then, he tries to understand the clock and the use of the clock in terms of the foot-rule and the water-meter and their use. It is this comparison which leads to the idea of something like linoleum, and something like water, and it is something like linoleum and something like water that he looks for in the neighborhood of the clock. Finding nothing, he is troubled and says that he does not know what time is.

I have noticed in this explanation that we measure linoleum, water, and time. This means that there is an extensive parallel in the language of these. We use numbers in respect to each, and, of course, there are units. In measuring we do some things that are similar. We read off numbers on the foot-rule, on the face of the clock, on the face of the water-meter, and, of course, we add, subtract, etc. Naturally it doesn't follow that one can answer such questions as: How many square feet of linoleum in one hour? or how much water in five minutes? If someone insisted that he did not know what an hour is because he could not say how many square feet of linoleum there are in an hour, then, in any case, you would see what it was that he did not know. And so with how much water in five minutes. Now what I have noticed here is a relatively uninteresting illustration of the way in which the language of time is intertwined with the language of quite different contexts. This intertwining of the language gives rise to something like the experience one may have when a familiar street in one neighborhood leads one without one's being aware into a neighborhood which is of a quite different character. From the village into the Italian section, from this busy square into a street of quiet houses and gardens. A different world! This may be entertaining. It may also be quite confusing and distressing. "I'm lost. Where am I?" So too with the language of time. Stepping, as it were, on one word and pressing it hard, loosing it from its present context, one may suddenly find oneself stepping along in a different context, scarcely knowing where one is, and then thoroughly confusing neighborhoods. In the city the view of one bit of street by which one came into the different neighborhood may mislead one into supposing he hasn't left the other neighborhood at all and so he may continue to try to find his way within this neighborhood as he well might in the other. This is dizzying. It may be like trying to find your way in a strange house, in the middle of the night, when you are not enough awake to realize you are not at home. So you blink and bump your head.

In what immediately follows I am going to present an heterogeneous grouping of fragments of the intertwining of the language of time with the language or languages of other things. There will be nothing systematic about this. There will be fragments, sentences or phrases, which will be like short streets connecting neighborhoods. There will be others in which I enter the adjacent neighborhood. The point of this will be to provide further illustration of that aspect of language which, when taken in a certain absentminded way, may give one's head a permanent whirl, or when taken in a certain well-lit mindedness, may give one a ride not unlike that one gets in a fun-house.

Notice the variety and color: Once upon a time. He's behind time but four steps ahead of Jones. A long time ago. There's been a mix-up in time. A time interval. Can you tell time? I wouldn't if I could. Time is mean. Mean-time. The clock is striking the hour. Savagery in the belfry. Time passed. So did the milk-man. The time is up. Night fell. No wonder, it's so dark! In a twinkling. In the shake of a lamb's tail. Shorter than the shake of a puppy's tail. The turn of the century. The turn of the screw. The turn of a phrase. It will soon be time. What was it before? A month of Sundays. Five minutes late. Which five minutes? Times overlap. It seams so. He lives in the past. He dies in the future. Time is money. What's money? Money is groceries. Time is groceries. Right now. Wrong hereafter. Relativity of time and morals. On the hour. Shove over about five minutes. The crowded years. Squeeze in a little time. Time slips away. Between the hours of four and six. Ah! There you are! A stitch in time. A gap in the years. Time heals all things. Remove the stitches. The fulness of time. The fulness of skirts. Time takes its toll. Toll pays for highways. "Time hath a wallet at her back." Nevermore. Nevertheless. Always the same. The day is shot. "Who killed cock-robin?" Not yet? No, yet. Pause for a second. The second is late. No duel without a second. No duo without a second. Take your time. Why does he get a larger piece? Down the corridors of time. Electric light and running water for the first fifty years. "Looking backwards." A time capsule. For chronic diseases. To counter-act the acids of modernity. Chrono-Belcher. A secure tomorrow. Yesterday teetering on the verge of 12 p.m. The future "in a retrospective arrangement." The past teaches us. The lessons of the past. "There, that will teach you to keep your hands out of the fire." The past teaching all hands present to mind future fires. The best time of the year. The dancing hours. Compline hour. The hour of decision. Tossed coin. All heads saying, "Tails." Time to eat. Chronic gluttony. Stuffing yourself, gobbler. Fat as a tick. Spare me a tidbit, just a tasty interval. Time consuming. Just a minute for desert. Time to turn over a new leaf. From the palm in my hand to the tree taking leaf in the spring.

And now I should like to nimble-numble at a few of these. "*Once upon a time.*" Indeed! Twice below a certain space we met. In the subway. You said: "Have you the time?" And I said: "I have fifty years." You pouted. It was about time you, a pout about. "*He's behind time.*" What a pity! He can never catch up. Time cannot be overtaken. No overtaking. And he with his future always just a jiffy ahead of him, and he crying, "Halt! Halt!" "*A long time ago.*" A far country. Go back in time some place, and live in those other people's presents. Go to bed in 1953 and get up in time to buy corn from Joseph in Egypt. "Is your name Benjamin?" "No, no, sir. I did not steal your silver-cup. I have just dreamed in from the U.S.A." He would not understand. "You are under arrest. You are an anachromist. When do you come from? How did you get out of your century?" Meeting Caesar there too, asking Joseph for a few husks and a bucket of ashes to celebrate the Ides of Kislev. "What language do you speak?" "Dico the Roman language," he says in his very best Egyptian which is English. "It was once going to be the most up-to-date, by jabberers, before the future returned." Joseph goes on filling sacks as though time had been renewed and tomorrow was still to come. "There's been a mix-up in time." Tangles in tense. A tense wood. Was issing and will and soon wassing. Ex post factos ante factoring. Eternal recurrence in a jumble. What are your whenabouts? "*The clock is striking the hour.*" A careless hour, loitering on the way to ten o'clock. Came in with chiming morning face, like snail, unwillingly to gong. Ten strokes on his pendulum. Doing time.

There are good times, corking good times, uncorking good times. ("A barrel of fun," "a barrel of monkeys.") There are bad times, perfect times, dandy times, nice times, high old times, hard times, grand times, gay times, sad times, rotten times, times that are out of joint. There's railroad time, Greenwich time, five-o'clock shadow on the sun-dial, exact time. We have, we make, we spend, we gain, we buy, we save, we sell, we put in, we waste, we while away ("wit a whittle whittle stick"). We give, we fill, we take out, we steal, we shorten, we squeeze out, we spare, we stretch, we lengthen, we cut, we halve, we keep, we hoard, we get, we take, we seize, we use, we watch, we pick up, we lack, we find, we need, we divide, we lose, we fritter away, we kill, we beat, we invest. What? Time. Time is money. Put time in the bank. Invest weekly. He, taking up his gun, said:

"I'm going out to kill time." She shuddered. Expert marksman. Catching time on the wing. But time flies. Time runs, time flows, time creeps ("Tomorrow and tomorrow and tomorrow ...to the last syllable..."), time never stops, time marches on (clopperty, clopperty, clop). Time waits for no man always at the same speed, twenty-fours every so many minutes.

Time is pressing. With a mangle, alas! ("And at my back I always hear.") Time withers. (Wrong. "Time cannot wither nor custom stale.") Time corrupts. The prey of time, the ravages of time. The prisoners of time. ("Stone walls... nor iron bars ..." but....) One solid hour. Packed with thrills. Room for only one more bubble. Time is a blabber. Time will tell. A lost week-end. Found in the middle of no-when, a tiny island surrounded by something like water. Free time. "The gift of another day." The space of one week. How to compute the area of one week with two unknowables. My time is yours. I have a second. Let's split. A split second. Sounds like a cocoa-nut. Nothing inside. A light-year. A dark hour. Signs of the times: Neon, jitters, robins, whirring, falling leaves, squirrels hiding nuts. Working against time. ("Give me a lever long enough and a fulcrum strong enough..." and I'll stop everything.) Time hangs heavy. Ripe bananas. Seize the moment. By the scruff of the nick of time. A time-piece. "Slab of eternity." A chip off the old block universe. Times without number. Times with number: Three times three. In a trice. In a tricecycle, over and over and over. He came in on time. Time is faster than a horse.

The time is coming. (Have you had word? Travel plans.) The time is near. ("I can hear the whistle blowing.") The time is here. (Bring out the red carpet.) The time is going. (All aboard!) The time is gone. (Disappearing in the shadows.) Yesterday is but a shadow of its former self. You'd scarcely know it was the same day. So changed. Been through something. Do you remember the time? Indeed. I'd recognize it anywhere. Is it long since? My last haircut. Travel by memory. Make it in no time at all. See the world from a howdah decked out by your own "imagicnation." A week's work. Six working days, everybody else sitting around. Five-day week. Seventy-some in a year. The first day of the week fell on a Sunday. That's why Sunday walks bowed. Many happy returns of the day. Recurrence to suit wishes. Same day last year this year. Eat the same cake, burn the same candle at the other end. In one year and out of the other. A full day, brimming over, spilled. My time is exhausted. Breathless. Can't stand the pace. A blue Monday, a white Christmas, a black day in our history, "the violet hour," "rosy-fingered dawn," a golden age, the faded past, a green morning, dark ages, the mauve decade, a gray day, a pretty soon, a handsome present, a bright future. Time in assorted colors. Velvet night. What color is Tuesday? Tuesday is fat and florid.

There's no time like the present. There are no apples like the apples of my eye. There's no space like here. "There's no place like home." Never postpone today. Postpone tomorrow. When? Tomorrow. But I may not have the time. That's just the time to postpone. A sentence of five years. Parse it. An exercise for logicians who live a thousand years. A compound proposition. For ever and a day. A baker's dozen. A billion years. The story of the rocks. "Once upon a glacial morning, before the sun rose; there was no sun....." The crucible of time. Hot. Rag-time.

A man on his way lost time. His watch also lost time. A double loss! Time lost cannot be recovered. Like spilled milk. Sop it up. Ten minutes in a wet towel. "Little Sheba." Another man found time, but not the time the other man lost. Ten minutes as good as new, unused, second-hand. Second-hand time goes faster. He also found one dime and he found some things impossible. When he said that he had found some things impossible, people would not believe him. They said no one could find things impossible, that there are no impossible things. Time, they allowed, was possible, and when they asked him where he found time, he said time was up and wouldn't say another word. They figured that what is up must come down and so they waited. Time would find them out. They winced at the thought. Then the man who found time turned, elbowing his way through time, he was virtually in time, and said to the man who had lost time, "My time is yours," and so finder shared with loser, the ten minutes he had found, breaking it into two five-minute time-pieces. They tick-talked to one another until time ran out on them. Surprised, they both exclaimed, "Where has the time gone?" One answered, "South, for the winter," but the other answered: "No, time is up again. It was high time, you know. It went past like that." And he pretended that he was a bird. "Of course," said the other, "Time flies, have you never heard of the mosquito fleet? but will time return?" "No," said the other, "Time is no homing pigeon." And they were very sad, as they both stood, looking up, watching time flapping its wings in the avisphere.

These are "the fragments I have shared" in order to prepare myself for what I propose to do in the next section. These fragments, you may remember, I intended as further illustration of the intertwining of the language of time with the language or languages of other things. Obviously this intertwining may be exploited sportingly. My interest is in the fact that there is this intertwining. And my interest comes about in this way. There are cases in which this intertwining has serious consequences, and in which it is difficult to see both what the intertwining in a particular case is, and that the serious consequences do arise from such intertwining. The serious consequence I have in mind is that a man should say, "I do not know what time is."

III

In this section I want to study a second case of the man who does not know what time is, this case a bona-fide one, a case with which I have wrestled. The case is expressed in the following long sentence: "The great mystery of Time, were there no other; the illimitable, silent, never-resting thing called Time, rolling, rushing on, swift, silent, like an all-embracing ocean-tide, on which we and all the universe swim like exhalations, like apparitions which are and then are not; this is forever very literally a miracle; a thing to strike us dumb,—for we have no word to speak about it." "The great mystery of Time." I propose now to try to understand just what it is that is the mystery of time by way of certain other mysteries. Time is not the only mystery. There is the mystery of the sea and there is the mystery of the sky and stars. There are, of course, minor mysteries such as the mystery of caves and of deep places. And man too, it is said, is a mystery, the greatest mystery of all. For the present I wish to consider the mystery of the sea and that of the sky and stars. I am no doubt led to these in particular by the language in which the mystery of time is expressed. I turn first to the mystery of the sea.

Consider, then, some thoughtful man in the days of Columbus or some days before Columbus, as he looks out to the west from some high rock on the shore of the great ocean. He ponders that endless expanse of water, water, water, and more water, on and on, water, wave upon wave, never-ending. Is there another shore? A shoreless sea! His eyes find no relief. There is only water. He stomps with his foot on the rock, with a relish for terra firma. He turns his gaze upon the hills behind him, his eyes resting there, a refuge from the terrors of endlessness. "Are there hills like these there?" and he fixes his eyes steadily on the west. He imagines himself winged like a bird, in flight over the water, arriving at another shore, strange peoples, palm trees, rich meadows, a better land, who knows? "Giants, perhaps, with walrus mustaches. And clusters of grapes borne between two upon a staff." This is not the first time he has stood upon this rock and mused upon the lands that are far away, washed by the water at his feet. There has been talk too, hushed and wonder-full, with friends, and even some levity. "Come, let's get into my little boat and we'll find the other shore." All for smile's sake. They knew and he knew that they would not venture out in any boat, big or little. Another shore? Might not their boat suddenly be carried by the strong waters, tumbling into the abyss, far away from mama and the kitchen stove? Leviathan is no house-cat. And even were the sea set in a saucer and all were well in quiet weather, might not some storm carry them all over the edge like spilled coffee to spatter the floor of the fundament? And so the sea teased them but they did not dare to attempt to pluck out the heart of its mystery. "Three wise men of Gotham!" One man did, of course. And, whether in unquiet desperation (furious at the infinite) or in quiet confidence, he set sail to set his eyes to rest upon that other who-knows-whether shore. On Columbus day! "There is another shore." And he looked back, following the line of the wake of his boat, and he thought of that rock on that other other shore.

Here, then, is a simple case of mystery. Is there another shore? Are there people there? (Is Mars inhabited? No, not yet. But there is a little clover growing out of the rocks.) There are questions, and wistfulness, and a certain helplessness. "We'll never find out." (What's at the end of the rainbow?) And then some brave sailor dares to face the terrors, and returns with a few gay feathers and an olive leaf and a piece of wampum. And that is the end of the mystery.

This is, however, by no means all of the mystery of the sea. Imagine the sea under a pale moon with clouds. Mystery has its own sky. "I should never have made the sun, but I should have made the moon. The sun is too bright." The moon is for vague and sweet wonder, the sea and waves in soft light and shadow. And things under the sea! The lost Atlantis, the submerged cathedral, Davy Jones' locker, lost ships, mermaids, and pirates' gold. "So is this great and wide sea, wherein are things creeping, innumerable, both small and great beasts." The sea is deep and is dark and wide, and swarms with tiny lights, the lanterns of little fishes. Oh! for a walk in that dark deep on the ocean floor to see the strange creatures like living gold and silver, treasures of the sea. The whale's home. "As we have seen, God came upon him in the whale, and swallowed him down to the living gulfs of doom, and with swift slantings tore him along 'into the midst of the seas,' where the eddying depths sucked him ten fathoms down, and 'the weeds were wrapped about his head' and all the watery world of woe bowled over him." "Ten fathoms down... the watery world of woe." And there are storms at sea and darkness and fog and rain and a thousand ships tossing under the stars. The Ancient Mariner, The Flying Dutchman, the man without a country, Captain Carlson on the broken ship!

And now notice this echo of the sentence which I quoted above: "The great mystery of the Sea, where there no other: the illimitable, noisy, never-resting thing we call The Sea, rolling, rushing on, swift, noisy, an all-embracing ocean, on which we and all the earth swim like exhalations, like apparitions which are and then are not; this is, forever, literally a miracle; a thing to strike us dumb,—for we have no word to speak about it."

This, I think, will not do. But I should like to notice the divergence in the following elaboration, engaging still the language in which the original sentence goes on about time. Imagine this mediation: "The great mystery of the sea, were there no other," and he, the man on the rock, shakes his head slowly, sighs, and looks out upon the water. And he thinks of the stars. "The illimitable." He begins counting the waves for as far as he can see. He gives up, and looks out beyond the last wave he counted. "Noisy." The waves break upon the shore. "Listen! You hear the grating roar." "Never-resting thing we call the sea." "Sophocles long ago heard it on the Aegean." Not one drop of water in all this expanse is still, nor has ever been. "Endlessly rocking," as water falls rise, and water-rises fall, rocking water. "Rolling, rushing on, swift." His eyes catch one line of surf cresting one high wave and they follow its rising tumult, faster, faster, as it pursues the wave before it, swifter, swifter, till it dashes in foam upon the shore. He shouts "Stay! Stay!" and braces himself as with his eyes to halt the wild sea-horses, which rise and leap over his command. Testing his power! (King Canute went home pretty well soaked.) Tide waits and waves wait for no man, nor for any man's word or eye. "An all-embracing ocean." Three-fourths of the earth's surface is water and all the land is an island, floating on that all-encompassing sea. "On which" we and all that is on the earth and all the land, swim like flotsam and then some, like "mire and dirt" cast up by the troubled sea. Our land rests at anchor at the mercy of impervious, reckless water, sustained and shaken by an incontinent sea into whose depths, at the stir of one wild shudder, any windy day, it may fall down, down, down, whales scampering, itself to be dissolved, water to water. "This is forever very literally a miracle; a thing to strike us dumb, for we have no word to speak about it."

Now I should like to comment on this. I tried in the first place to represent the mystery of the sea, its overwhelming extent, its depths and darkness, the lore of history and story, the great beasts and shining little fishes, strange, unknown to man. The sea is full of mystery. My intention was to see whether I could, having had a glimpse of the mystery of the sea, write about that mystery in the words in which the sentence goes on about the mystery of time. Time is illimitable. Well, so is the sea of overwhelming extent. For the purposes of wonder it is large enough. "Silent?" No, not silent, but, then, perhaps noise has its own mystery. "Never-resting?" Indeed! the sea never rests. "Rolling, rushing, swift?" Yes, sometimes more spectacularly even than time. "An all-embracing ocean-tide?" You could say so. There's water all around us. And we and the universe exhalations, apparitions, swimming? No. And this in any case does not enter into the mystery of the sea. And now if we say that time like the sea is very big and very restless, "mighty like a whale," is time's mystery further like the mystery of the sea? The sentence takes no account of the light of the moon shining pale on time, no account of lost cities, lost ships, lore of history and story, submerged in time. Where are they now? At the bottom of the sea of time. It takes no account of "things creeping, innumerable," "of small and great beasts" hidden in the folds of time, time stretched out like a curtain. So far, then, I think we can say that comparing the mystery of time to the mystery of the sea helps on the whole chiefly to see that they are not similar, that one cannot understand the mystery of time in this way. Tentatively, let us say that both time and the sea are of marvelous extent and that both are restless.

There is another mystery, the mystery of sky and stars. Mystery is, of course, bound up with the unknown, with wonder. The mystery of the sea is articulate, but the mystery of sky and stars is relatively inarticulate. There are no such questions as: Is there another shore? If I go straight up, will I bump my head? The question, in any case, hasn't the right tone. The sky is not strewn with lost ships, with pirates' gold, with a lost Atlantis. If on occasion a great church were suddenly whirled off the earth into space and we saw it disappearing in the direction of a far star, intact, not a brick out of place, and if men now and then were caught in a draught, waved good-bye from a cloud, and we saw them ride off for a spree among the stars, or if we now and then saw or thought we saw in faintest outline the inter-stellar caravans moving swiftly, red and green lights flashing, before and after landing, then we should have something more like the mystery of the sea. Even such a question as: Is Mars inhabited? hasn't the right atmosphere, is generally unconnected with the mystery of the sky and stars. Wonder in this case is vague wonder. The sky and stars are too far away, and they have not swallowed, and have not hidden in their depths, treasure and the burnished lore of history and story. So our wonder has little substance. We do not look steadfastly at some star and ask: And are they singing a hymn in that church, high notes bouncing off the points of neighboring stars? Will Jonathan, who flew away yesterday, sift down a spray of star-dust to show Stella he hasn't forgotten?

Still, there is wonder.

Consider the verses:

> Twinkle, twinkle, little star!
> How I wonder what you are!
> Up above the world so high
> Like a diamond in the sky.

Little stars are cherished shining in the wonder of children and children's wonder twinkles in the winkles of the star.

And now this from a man who did not write nursery rhymes: "Two things there are fill the mind with ever new and increasing admiration and awe, the oftener and more steadily we reflect on them: the starry heavens above and the moral law within." " The more steadily we reflect on them!" Did Kant on his walk one day look into the sky and at one bright star and say: "How I wonder what you are!" I suppose not. He looked into "The starry heavens above," and reflected. And what were his words? Did he say: "And behold the height of the stars, how high they are," or "When I consider thy heavens, the work of thy fingers, the moon and stars which thou hast ordained, what is man that thou art mindful of him?" Only, I take it, as we connect the stars with man, for instance, or with God, is there any richness in this mystery of the stars. St. Augustine's feeling, not only towards the heavens, but also towards the earth and sea is expressed in the following passage:

And what is this? I asked the earth; and it answered, "I am not He." And whatsoever are therein made the same confession. I asked the sea and the deeps, and the creeping things that lived and they replied, "We are not thy God; seek higher than we." I asked the breezy air, and the universal air with its inhabitants answered, "Anaximenes was deceived, I am not God." I asked the heavens, sun, moon, and stars: "Neither," say they, "are we the God whom thou seekest." And I answered unto all those things which stand about the door of my flesh: "Ye have told me concerning my God that ye are not He; tell me something about Him." And with a loud voice they exclaimed, "He made us." My questioning was my observing of them; and their beauty was their reply.

The mystery of the stars is, I take it, something special, bathed in a religious light. There are descriptions of the heavens which are, however, quite different. Notice:

This most excellent canopy, the air, look you; this brave o'erhanging firmament, this majestical roof fretted with golden fire—why it appears no other thing to me than a foul and pestilent congregation of vapors.

And this:

> And that inverted bowl they call the sky
> Whereunder crawling cooped we live and die,
> Lift not your hands to It for help for it
> As impotently moves as you and I.

And this:

> A wise man
> Watching the stars pass across the sky,
> Remarked:
> In the upper air the fireflies move more slowly.

AMY LOWELL

And in these the note of mystery is gone.

Apart from the religious overtones, however, some men have spoken of the mystery of the heavens in a different vein, almost literally of that mystery as a form of consternation. It comes, I think, to something like this. There are forms of picture-puzzle arrangements of black dots, for instance, on a white background, and the puzzler is invited to make out the picture of an old man brushing his shoes or of a bear with his head in a jar. If he cannot make it out, then, of course, the arrangement remains a mystery. Now, then, it is supposed that if the stars were arranged all over the blue himmels in a network of squares, then there would be no mystery. No one would then be fascinated by the stars. It might in that case be very monotonous and any-one who suggested that the stars should be redistributed as if scattered out of a pepper-pot might be acclaimed as a fine architect of the new heavens. Nevertheless this deep-seated hankering for a pattern has this consequence, that when men now do look into the star-lit skies they are overwhelmed and baffled as by a puzzle which exceeds their capacities. They do, of course, find what relief they can in the big and little dipper and the lady in a chair, the arrow and the little fox and so on. The aim however is one picture and it is the frustration involved here which is expressed in the idea of the mystery. The fascina-tion remains, even after one has given up. A variant of this idea is that when one looks into the sky he is tempted straightway to count them, this, perhaps, being one way of arranging them. But he cannot. Hence, the following comment of Burke:

> The number is certainly the cause. The apparent disorder augments the grandeur, for the appearance of care is highly contrary to our idea of magnificence. Besides the stars lie in such apparent confusion as makes it impossible on ordinary occasions to reckon them. This gives them the advantage of a certain infinity.

So it is in various ways the overspreading "heaven-tree of stars," the everlasting chandelier in the ceiling of the world feeds our wonder.

And now reflect: "The great mystery of the Heavens, were there no other; the illimitable, silent, never-resting thing called the Heavens, rolling, rushing on, swift, silent, like an all-embracing ocean-tide on which we and all the universe swim like exhalations, like apparitions which are and then are not; this is forever very literally a miracle; a thing to strike us dumb,—for we have no word to speak about it." Will this do?

I am trying to understand "the mystery of Time," meaning by this that I am trying to understand the man who speaks of such a mystery. The clues to understanding him may be such other mysteries as we are acquainted with, and, of course, what he goes on to say. It is in this way that I came to remind myself of the mysteries of sea and sky. The language in which the author of the sentence writes of the mystery certainly encourages this. We have already seen that this may throw some light upon the mystery. Time is "an all-embracing ocean-tide." Strange sea! If one could paddle with one's feet on the bank of time as one can paddle on the bank of the sea, then, surely, a part of time would be laid. As it is, we know that we do paddle with our feet in the stream of time, but we cannot feel it. No one stubs his toe there against the current. As for what I have noted of the mystery of the heavens and stars, there is even less that is useful in understanding "the mystery of time." There is nevertheless something else which may be described as the mystery of the heavens which may be useful and which is analogous to the idea of "the strange sea." I should like to return to this, but before I do so, I want to study more closely the "description" of time in the sentence about the mystery.

It is clear that no one has come to think of time as like the sea or like the sky, by having seen both time and the sea or sky, as one might have come to think of the sky as like the sea. For we do see both sea and sky. But, then, the question is as to how we do come to think of time as like the sea. The answer is, I take it, simple enough. The same types of sentence which serve us in discussing time or in remarks about (?) time, serve us also in describing the sea. It is this similarity which gives rise to the illusion that time is a sea.

The sentences that I want to notice are these:

> Time is illimitable.
> Time is silent.
> Time never rests.
> Time rolls, rushes on.
> Time is all-embracing.

I propose with respect to each of these sentences, first of all to explain briefly the use of the sentence, and then to go on to show how by assimilating the meaning of the sentence to somewhat parallel sentences about the sea, we come up with the stirring meta-mystery of time. My explanation of the use of these sentences will very likely be incomplete and may be incorrect. My intention, however, is to exhibit the character of that use, sufficiently to distinguish its use from the analogous sentences about the sea.

Time is illimitable. What does this mean? Briefly, this means that for such expressions as "The first hour," "the last hour," "the beginning of time," "the end of time," we have, save in certain contexts such as "the first hour of the day," "during the last hour," no use. This involves further that we also have no use for such sentences as "there is no first hour" and "there is no last hour." We may all recollect how St. Augustine wrestled . with this.

The temptation, however, to try to understand this in a different way is exceedingly strong. "If the roving thought of anyone should wander through the images of by-gone times," then one may go on as follows. Beyond the present moment, there is a next, and a next and a next. Tomorrow is coming, and next week, and January and 1955. And then? Then another decade, another century. And the same thing will be the case if you look behind you over this present moment's shoulder. There is the moment before and so on and on. There is yesterday and last week and September and 1953. And then? Then the forties, and 1900. And, of course, you can go on indefinitely, tearing the leaves off old calendars and making new ones. A shoreless sea! Isn't this how it is at sea when you stand high and look over the water, the sea before you, wave upon wave, dimming into the waters of tomorrow and the waters of yesterday? Is not every man a Flying Dutchman until the sea of time swallows him? There is no shore, no harbor. Time is illimitable.

Time is silent. This is a remarkable detail, and is emphasized by repetition in the sentence quoted at the beginning of this part of the essay. Consider. Time passes. Listen! You could hear a pin drop. "Like a thief in the night." (Time is a thief. It steals your youth away. "Gather ye rose-buds while ye may." "Time, you old gypsy man!") Time passes. There's not a squeak. Helmholtz could not have heard it. The highest fidelity cannot capture it. On cat's paws! Keep your ear to space, catch an echo as time bangs against the earth's axis, a faint throbbing. The sea is not silent. As the waves pound one another, they roar; but time hasn't even a tiny cry. It is also true, of course, that time is not blue, does not smell of fish, and tastes neither salty nor of lemon-ade. Why, then, is a special point made of this, that time is silent? Well, I take it that if one has already got an impression of time as like the sea, and one has in mind too its restlessness and its rolling, then the silence of such a sea intensifies the mystery. Imagine a sea, a turbulent sea, silent as a picture. Is not that a strange sea?

I need, perhaps, not remark that, apart from conversations

between two men, neither of whom knows what time is, the sentence: "Time is silent," has no point. Neither is space sour.

Time never rests. It's never an hour for more than sixty minutes. That's how it is with now, too. Now always comes in at the same time, now, that is, and moves on. Guests may stay on, but four o'clock leaves on schedule. Tomorrow is coming, moves in, moves on, is gone, joins yesterday. It will never come by this way again. Time does not stand still. Nor does tomorrow come in, move out, and then rest. It keeps on going and every day it's farther away. There is no siesta, no rest, for time. Time marches on. Time waits for nobody. "Sun, stand thou still upon Gibeon; and thou moon, in the valley of Ajalon," was not spoken to Time. Time goes on, unwearied, what endurance! unwearying, without a break. Perpetual motion. Nothing can keep time back. Time is irresistible. Put your foot out on the last of Monday to halt Tuesday, and Tuesday runs, subtly rilling, over and through your foot. Get your foot wedged in between 4:59 and 5:01 and see it carried away, disappearing in the mists of last week. King Canute, throwing time back, buckets full of today hitting him full in the face as he tries to make tomorrow stand still. Too much pressure. Build a wall to keep the future out of this year. Make a lunge, telescoping time, jamming 4000 years into a 1000-year space. The engineering feat of the milleniums. The latest advances in Chronodamnamics. Working against time. Hopeless! Time rolls, rushes on, pushed on by the wave of the future. Against the sea you can build a wall. The sea has a bed. It does not rest but can rest. But time has no bed. Its waves are dashed against no shore. There is no shore. The past recedes every day another day. The future advances every day another day. This is, shall we say, an eternal fact, as old as calendars.

So, in this case, there never will be a Columbus who will set sail to explore and to discover the shore from which the future starts out. The future, no matter how far into tomorrow-orroworrow he will have advanced, will already be on its way. Time will not be caught napping.

Time is all-embracing. Everything is in time. When is four o'clock? In time. When did Socrates live? In time. When will you keep still? In time. How can time hold so much? Time is very big. The fishes are in the water. The ships are in the sea. The stars are in the sky. The birds are in the air. And all things, fishes and water, and birds and air, and stars and sky are in time. Time is immense. Without water fish cannot swim. Without air birds cannot fly. Without sky the stars cannot shine. The water carries the fish, the air carries the birds. The sky carries the stars. Water, air, and sky are buoyant. And water and air and sky are themselves buoyant, buoyed, in buoyantest time. Time is all embracing, all-embuoyant. And if, now, everything is in time, is time also in all things? Are not all things time-embracing? Mutual love! It is so. Time permeates all things. Lift the tiny scales of little fishes, time is there. Examine the entrails of birds, time is there. Tiresias knew. And in the hottest regions of the stars, time is there. In the drop of water, in the breath of air, in a patch of sky, time is there. Time permeates all things. And now we can also understand the words: "on which we and all the universe swim." For as fish swim in the water and birds swim in the air and the stars swim in the sky, so all swimming in the water and all swimming in the air and all swimming in the sky are swimmings in time, the sea, air, sky, of time. Time is a sea, an air, a sky.

And now, I think that we are near to plucking out the heart of the mystery of time. But we are still to explain the rest of that part of the sentence which begins: "on which we and all the universe swim." It goes on: "like exhalations, like apparitions which are and then are not." Time's exhalation, apparitions of time! For this purpose I should like to quote the following sentences from Sir Isaac Newton, from which it will, I think, be clear that the mystery of time is twin to the mystery of the aether.

But to proceed to the hypothesis: It is to be supposed therein, that there is an aetherial medium, much of the same constitution with air, but far rarer, subtler, and more strongly elastic.... But it is not to be supposed that this medium is one uniform matter, but composed partly of the main phlegmatic body of aether, partly of other various aetherial spirits, much after the manner that air is compounded of the phlegmatic body of air, intermixed with various vapours and exhalations. For the electric and magnetic effuvia, and the gravitating principle seem to argue such variety. Perhaps the whole frame of nature may be nothing but various contextures of some certain aetherial spirits or vapours, condensed as it were by precipitation, much after that manner that vapours are condensed into water, or exhalations into grosser substances, though not so easily condensable; and after condensation wrought into various forms, at first by the immediate hand of the creator, and ever since by the power of nature, which by virtue of the command, increase and multiply, became a complete imitation of the copy set by the Protoplast. Thus, perhaps, may things be originated from aether.

So the aether too is an all-embracing sea or atmosphere, a medium like air, and to it are related "vapours and exhalations," as to time are related exhalations and apparitions. "Thus, perhaps, may all things be originated from aether," as on time, "we and all the universe swim, like exhalations, like apparitions." And now as there is a mystery of the aether so to there is a mystery of time. For the aether, though much like air, is "rarer, subtler, and more strongly elastic," and whereas one can paddle in the water with one's feet, and one can hold out one's hand in a breeze, the aether goes right through one's foot and hand. One can catch neither touch nor sight of it. Besides it is silent. Also there are the mysteries of vapours and exhalations, of precipitation and condensation. And so the mystery of time is analogous. Is not time also "rarer, subtler" and perhaps "more strongly elastic" than air, and, perhaps, even than aether? It is difficult, perhaps, to say whether the mystery of time in the sentence quoted is the same as the mystery of aether or whether it is the mystery of a medium even rarer and subtler than aether of which the aether itself is an exhalation, a gross form. On the latter assumption there is this order of media: water, air, aether, time. In any case, the following sentence is not an unreasonable parody: "The great mystery of Aether, were there no other; the illimitable, silent, never-resting thing called aether" (notwithstanding its phlegmatism), "rolling, rushing on, swift" (these words show the traces of the analogy with the sea, but wind also rushes), "silent, like an all-embracing ocean-tide, on which we and all the universe swim like exhalations, like apparitions which are and then are not; this is forever literally a miracle; a thing to strike us dumb, for we have no word to speak about it."

So we can understand this case of a man who does not know what time is, as like that of the man who does not know what aether is. He is like one who breathes deeply to take one big breath of time, hoping to get wind of it in this way. And he would like to know how out of so much time and a trowel to make a star.

There, now I think I know what it is that this man who does not know what time is, does not know. He also did not get the drift.

REFLECTIONS ON MOORE'S RECENT BOOK*

I SHOULD LIKE IN THESE PAGES to think about this book in terms of the following passage from the first chapter. The first chapter is entitled "What is Philosophy?" And the passage quoted is a part of Moore's answer to that question.

> To begin with, then, it seems to me that the most important and interesting thing which philosophers have tried to do is no less than this; namely: To give a general description of the *whole* of the universe, mentioning all the most important kinds of things which we know to be in it, considering how far it is likely that there are in it important kinds of things which we do not absolutely know to be in it, and also considering the most important ways in which these kinds of things are related to one another. I will call this, for short, "Giving a general description of the *whole* universe," and hence will say that the first and most important problem of philosophy is: To give a general description of the *whole* universe.

I propose now to study these sentences both in order to grasp the conception of philosophy that determines the inquiry in this book and in order to understand how some parts of this

* G. E. Moore, *Some Main Problems of Philosophy* (New York: Macmillan, 1953).

book are related to the attempt described in this passage. First I want to study it in terms of a part of what Moore offers as such a description. My main interest will be in the phrase "the most important kinds of things which we know to be in it," and of that phrase, especially the phrase "kinds of things."

So I want first to attend to the words, "description" and "the most important kinds of things." Ordinarily a man describes what he has seen, for someone else who has not seen. And what in any place or time are "the most important kinds of things" will depend upon a man's needs or interests. So, for instance, travelers and explorers when they return home tell their friends about what they have seen. And they do not tell about everything but only about what excited their surprise and admiration. The following passage from *Robinson Crusoe* will illustrate this:

> It was on the 15th of July that I began to take a more particular survey of the island itself. I went up the creek first, where, as I hunted, I brought my rafts on shore. I found after I came about two miles up that the tide did not flow any higher, and that it was no more than a little brook of running water, very fresh and good: but this being the dry season, there was hardly any water in some parts of it—at least, not enough to run in any stream, so as it could be perceived. On the bank of this brook, I found many pleasant savannahs or meadows, plain, smooth, and covered with grass; and on the rising parts of them, next to the higher grounds, where the water, as might be supposed, never overflowed, I found a great deal of tobacco, green, and growing to a great and very strong stalk. There were divers other plants, which I had no notion of understanding about, that might, perhaps, have virtues of their own, which I could not find out. I searched for the cassava root.... I saw large plants of aloes.... I saw several sugar canes.... [The next day I] found different fruits, and particularly I found melons upon the ground in great abundance and grapes upon the trees.

It won't do, of course, to say that Robinson Crusoe *tried* to give a description of a part of the island. Perhaps he never tried at all. He just described. And he mentioned some at least of the most important kinds of things which he saw "to be in it," running water, pleasant savannahs, tobacco, aloes, sugar-cane, melons, and grapes. As for the cassava root, he searched for that, and presumably thought it likely that there was some. Robinson Crusoe was, of course, a sailor and wrote down such notes as these for people who did not leave home.

Gulliver, such another sailor, on the sixteenth day of the previous month, June, though not at all in that same year, also ventured forth upon a strange island. He observed "the country all barren and rocky" and observed also "a huge creature," and "the length of grass, which in those grounds that seemed to be kept for hay, was about twenty-foot high." As in the case of Robinson Crusoe, Gulliver too did not try to describe. He described. He was English, could write, and he had seen clearly what there was, or at least some of what there was, in the island. It perhaps never occurred to him before he saw that "huge creature" and that tall grass that there were such things in the island. At any rate, that he should tell about kinds of things so "important" is not surprising.

Are Moore's philosophers, then, such men as Robinson Crusoe and Gulliver? Are they men who have traveled far, and are their eyes and hearts full of strange and new things, and are they eager to tell the world? Are we perhaps to think of the philosopher as like those who have penetrated the jungles and who have seen what only those see who exercise themselves with "deep penetration" of wilderness and swamps? For the moment I say, "Well, why not?" But before making up our minds about this, let us notice Moore's explanation. Moore explains what it is that philosophers try to do by an example, an example, that is, of a description, such as a philosopher might give and, in part, such as Moore himself does give. The description is introduced as "certain views about the universe, which are held nowadays by almost everybody." This description goes on, in part, as follows:

To begin with, then, it seems to me we certainly believe that there are in the universe enormous numbers of material objects of one kind or another.... But now, ... we believe also that there are in the universe certain phenomena very different from material objects. In short, we believe that we men, besides having bodies, also have minds, and one of the chief things we mean by saying we have minds, is, I think, this, namely, that we perform certain mental acts of consciousness.... These things, these acts of consciousness are certainly not themselves material objects. And yet we are quite certain that there are immense numbers of them.

You will notice at once that what is here called a description is something quite different from those descriptions cited above from Robinson Crusoe and Gulliver. If when they returned home, and friends gathered at the harbor, eager to hear, if then, I say, Robinson Crusoe or Gulliver had said, "Well, there were enormous numbers of material objects, and many acts of consciousness," it is not unlikely that some of their eager friends would have gone home disappointed. And if someone had shouted from the back of the crowd, "What! no tobacco, no melons, no grapes, no huge creature, no grass twenty-foot high?" and Robinson Crusoe had replied, "Perhaps—we noticed material objects and those things you mentioned are all material objects, so there might well have been such things," would not that have been a strange thing to hear? And notice too how different is the idea of important kinds of things. Fresh water is important if you are thirsty. And fruit is important if you are hungry. And a huge creature is important if you do not want to be eaten or stepped on. But, in this instance, Moore shows no special interest in tobacco, nor in fruit, nor in huge creatures. There are material objects. But not as though he would say, "Oh, what would we do without them!" In this book Moore seems much interested in the number of whatever the kind is that he is speaking of. There are "enormous numbers of material objects," "immense numbers" of acts of consciousness, "an immense number of propositions," a "number of truths...

enormously greater," "enormous numbers of universals," "an immense number of different specks of pure white," "tremendous numbers of them," "many millions of the most obvious facts," and "the number of spots in which no act of consciousness is taking place is immensely larger than that of those in which an act of consciousness is taking place." But the number, of whatever it is, is very likely neither the measure of importance nor the importance itself.

I have been interested up to this point in a certain similarity and a certain contrast between what travelers do and what philosophers do. The similarity may be seen in comparing the following two sentences. What do travelers do? They give a general description of the lands they have visited, (a part of the universe) mentioning all the most important kinds of things they have seen. What do philosophers do? They give a general description of the whole of the universe, mentioning all the most important kinds of things they know to be in it. Now one might suppose that philosophers do for the whole universe what each traveler does for some part. So a philosopher's book might include excerpts from the writings of travelers. His book might be a compendium of travel literature. We know, of course, that this is not the case. Or again one might suppose that what distinguishes the account of the traveler from that of the philosopher is a certain high degree of generality. It might be supposed that if a philosopher did not know that there are material objects then he might find this out by reading travel literature. For what are water, meadows, aloes, and sugar cane but material objects? And so too with acts of consciousness. For what are taking surveys and hunting and finding and perceiving and supposing and searching and understanding but acts of consciousness? This idea of what philosophers do might also seem to be confirmed by that part of the description which Moore cites as of the sort which philosophers have given. Nevertheless, this too would be a mistake. Who would listen to a traveler who talks like a philosopher? What is it that makes what the philosopher says alive when he says it? What is his interest?

In order to understand this I should like to revert to an aspect of what makes the traveler's account interesting. The traveler goes far away. He visits, and he tells about what others have not seen. He tells about what is covered by great distances, about what is hidden from eyes that stay at home. Let us say then that the traveler describes the hidden, and that this is also what the philosopher does. But the hidden is now obviously of a different sort; for whereas sailors sail the seas, the philosopher stays at home. I should like now to try to understand what it is that stirs the mind and heart of philosophers.

Before I go on to consider this, I should like to notice the role of what Moore calls "common-sense views." These are views "which are held nowadays by almost everybody," and include that part which I quoted above. It is obvious that Moore does not consider that material objects and acts of consciousness are hidden. Concerning them no special investigation is required and there are no doubts. Those views, however, are only a part of that description which, according to Moore, philosophers have tried to give, and in Moore's book they serve as a starting point for the discovery of other "important kinds of things." This is especially true of material objects, and our knowledge of them. For they serve in much the way that a Chinese box serves, which, if you examine it carefully, reveals other boxes hidden within it. That our knowledge of material objects should serve in this way, is, I take it, no part of the "common-sense" view. So we get in Moore's "description... mentioning all the most important kinds of things," not only those recognized by almost everybody, but also those hidden from almost everybody. And among those hidden kinds of things are sense-data, "material objects" (the hidden "material objects" are not to be confused with the material objects almost everybody knows), propositions, (which are, and later, in the book, cannot be) facts, truths, and universals. The interest in the hidden is common to children, to travelers, and to the philosopher. But the concept of the hidden which moves philosophers is nothing so simple as: "What's in that box?" or "Where are my spectacles?" or "Are there zebras with stripes running the other way in Tasmania?" If we can understand this, I think, we may better understand what Moore also tried to do in these lectures.

I should like now to explain the idea of the hidden. A squirrel hides nuts. A thief hides loot. The cloud hides the sun. A cunning person hides his motives. The children hide behind the door. Nature hides secrets. We look for what is hidden. We dig in the sand. We lift the mattress. We look behind the door. We study a man's face. We peer through foliage. We use microscopes. What I want to notice especially is that when we look for what is hidden we must know first of all *that* something is hidden. We must know what to look for. Sometimes this is very simple. We may see the squirrel hide nuts. We may see the children run to hide behind the door. We may hear a rustling in the bushes. Sometimes the case is by no means so simple. A man may look into his microscope to discover a germ, a parasite, which he has never seen, but which he knows "must" be there, just as an astronomer may look through his telescope to discover a planet, which he has never seen but which he knows "must" be there. Now, then, if the excitement of the philosopher is that of search, of discovery, and if this is relative to the hidden, what is it that has led him to search and to discover? Has he seen the squirrel hiding something? Has he heard a noise in the chimney? Does he have a theory which, like the theory of the man with the microscope and like the theory of the astronomer, leads him too to probe? Has he come upon a knothole in the fences of this world through which he looks intently, distinguishing in an obscure plenum silver lightnings whose form and motion he can scarcely make out? Are there silken threads, which as by accident he has laid his hand on, and which lead his tugging grasp to "things" on the other side to which the threads are attached? There are some things like knotholes in the fences of this world and some things like threads which lead the curious on and on. Beyond this, of course, looking intently through a knothole into a deep obscurity with flickerings of light, and tugging at a thread and hearing only the murmurs of the thread one tugs, may both be disappointing. It must be remembered that sometimes the hidden is not found. Among philosophers it sometimes happens that if one philosopher announces that he has discovered a new and "important kind of thing," some other may announce that there has been only a new and important kind of mistake. And he may write an essay on how to look through a knothole.

In what follows I propose to study several cases in which Moore in effect says: Here is another "important kind of thing." There are sense-data. There are "material objects." There are universals. In each case there will be something which I propose to call a clue, and a discovery. I am using the word clue in this case in a broad sense, so that even such things as knotholes and threads would be called clues. Anything is a clue, of course, only when taken in a certain way, and this is the conception I want to use. It is something which, taken in a certain way, leads to the discovery of sense-data, to the discovery of "material objects," or to the discovery of universals. It is especially the nature of these clues which I want to explore.

Moore, in the course of trying to give "a general description of the whole universe," mentions among "the most important kinds of things," sense-data. Most people who look, for instance, at an envelope, are unaware of sense-data. Some people, expert, and, as it were, with practiced eye, shall we say, discover them. Moore, of course, is such an expert. Now the case of sense-data is especially fascinating because though sense-data are to be discovered, yet they are represented as what one cannot help but see. How then can what one cannot help but see be hidden? Well, there are such things as the spectacles on your nose, cellophane, and the window you see through. For these too you may need a clue before you see them. Sense-data, like these, are hidden in full view, and yet not hidden like them. What then is the clue?

The clue to the presence of sense-data is a difference in the use of two such sentences as Moore cites in this "exhibition" of sense-data. The sentences are these: "The envelope is rectangular" and "The envelope looks like a rhombus." Moore, in the course of the exhibition, has held high in his right hand an envelope for all to see. Under these circumstances or similar ones these sentences and their uses are familiar to almost everybody. As Moore turns the envelope, though the envelope is rectangular, it now ceases to look rectangular. It looks like a rhombus. And isn't this now a strange thing, that when you keep your eye, as you suppose, fixed on the envelope, and you know very well that it does not change its shape, the envelope is not a caterpillar and is not a chameleon, nevertheless it now looks like a rhombus? What can have happened? What can have got in the way? This is the form of the question by which Moore introduces the conception of sense-data: "What exactly is it that happens when (as we should say) we see a material object?" Is there from the point of view of some ideal perception a normal sort of eye trouble? If, for instance, the envelope looked rectangular from any point of view and no matter how it was turned, then we should never doubt that when we see the envelope we do see the envelope.

Consider this case. Someone holds up an envelope and asks you to look at it. You do so. Now he turns the envelope very slowly, and on the sly, invisibly, he slips between your eyes and the envelope, a piece of paper in the shape of a rhombus. He, then, asks you, "What does the envelope look like?" And you say, "It looks like a rhombus." He smiles and says, "No wonder!" and pulls out the piece of paper, and waves it before you. "This is what you saw." And he goes on to explain: "This is what happened when (as you should say) you saw the envelope. I slipped this between your eyes and the envelope." Now imagine, further, not that someone on the sly, invisibly, plays tricks on you whenever you look at an envelope, but imagine that your eyes, on the sly, invisibly, exude colored shapes, and that these hang in the air between your eyes and the envelope, masking the envelope whenever you look. This would, as you can see, make seeing very interesting, but on the other hand, it might also make seeing very exasperating, supposing you wanted really to get a look at the envelope. How exasperating this might be, if you bother to think of it, would be clear if you thought, not of your eyes doing this, a fatality to which you might be resigned, but of that sly one's doing it, some pestering genius with pieces of paper whom you cannot shake off.

I have elaborated this point because of a common ambiguity in speaking of sense-data. Someone might say, "Of course, there are sense-data," and he might go on to explain this as Moore did by holding up an envelope and saying, "Now it looks different, doesn't it? And that's all there is to it." What I intended to make clear in introducing the pieces of paper and the exudations is the conception of the sense-datum as a *thing*, and of the *intervention* of sense-data in perception. Sense-data are among those "most important kinds of things which we know to be in it" (the universe).

Now, I think, I am prepared to explain in what sense sense-data are hidden and have been discovered. It is clear that when someone normally looks at an envelope when an envelope is held up for him to see, he does not have any of the feelings that go with being cheated, as though when he looks at an envelope something always intervenes to obstruct his view. If one ever did get a bare-faced look at the envelope, then, of course, when a sense-datum intervened he might immediately sense the difference and realize that something had gotten in the way. As it is, he never suspects any interference. If you ask him what he sees, he says that he sees an envelope, and if you ask him what it looks like, he says that it looks like a rhombus. And he has an explanation for that too. It's the way you're holding it. Now, then, what is hidden from him is what Moore describes as "What happens when" he sees an envelope. What happens when he sees an envelope is that he "sees" something else.

The question is: How, then, are sense-data, in the same sense in which they are also hidden, discovered? Clearly not as one might detect the frayed edges of a piece of paper, or a tear in the rhombus, or a shape not quite in place. Sense-data always fit an envelope like a glove and are nearly always in place. How then?

What is the clue? I am going to suggest one, which if it is not precisely the clue, will at any rate illustrate what I take the clue to be like. I suggested earlier that a clue is something which is taken in a certain way, and I also said that the clue in this instance is to be found in the difference in the use of two such sentences as "The envelope is rectangular" and "The envelope looks like a rhombus." It is now the latter of these two sentences which when taken in a certain way is the clue. This sentence when interpreted by analogy with another sentence which is very much like it, will lead straight to the conception of the sense-datum as a "thing" which intervenes in perception. Consider: If you put on the uniform of a policeman, then you will look like a policeman. Someone might even mistake you for a policeman and ask you the way to go home. And, then, of course, you would explain: "Oh, I'm not a policeman. I only look like a policeman. I'm only wearing these clothes." So you see, a man may look like a policeman, and an envelope may look like a rhombus. And how does a man come to look like a policeman? By wearing a policeman's clothes. And how does an envelope come to look like a rhombus? Well, by wearing, shall we say, the clothes of a rhombus? In any case, if in interpreting the sentence "The envelope looks like a rhombus" you follow the pattern of "He looks like a policeman," then the analogy will require a mask for the envelope. And how then could an envelope look like a rhombus? Naturally, by wearing the suitable mask. And this then is what it must do since it does look like a rhombus.

I was intent, you will remember, upon trying to understand the excitement of Moore's philosopher in terms of the conceptions of the hidden and the discovery of the hidden and the idea of the clue. The point of this was to understand also the use of the phrase, "the most important kinds of things." So I tried to identify the clue to the hidden and the now discovered sense-data, which are among "the most important kinds of things." Discovering sense-data is a little like discovering that what everyone, or "almost everybody," takes to be a forest and a running brook is a theatre set; and wouldn't that be something to write home about? But discovering sense-data is also much more like discovering that what everyone, or "almost everybody," takes to be the solid world, trees rooted in the earth and brooks running wet to the river, is an ever-shifting theatre set. And wouldn't that be something to cable home about? No wonder Moore's philosopher is excited. And the clue? It does not consist in anything like seams in the wallpaper, distinguished by looking closely. It consists rather in a peculiarity of certain sentences about what we see. Sentences similar to these and under other circumstances have other uses.

Moore also mentions "material objects" among the most important kinds of things in the universe. It may seem odd that Moore should have made a point of this since "almost everybody" would allow this, witness Robinson Crusoe and Gulliver. There would be some point in this if "material objects" also were hidden, and if, accordingly, they too had to be discovered. What this suggests is that there is some considerable ambiguity in the use of the expression "material objects," and there certainly is such ambiguity. Moore wrote: "To begin with, then, it seems to me, we certainly believe that there are in the universe enormous numbers of material objects of one kind or another." "We" is "almost everybody." I think we can understand this. If Moore, for instance, had held up an envelope and asked, "And what's this?" someone in the front row would have responded quite properly, "An envelope." And if he had gone on, smiling, "And is it a material object?" meanwhile snapping it with a finger, then, if someone had responded with, "Well, it isn't smoke. If you stick your finger through it, you'll tear it," Moore, too, might have regarded that as a good answer.

We can, perhaps, even imagine a situation in a company of "acts of consciousness" or "spirits," in which it would come as a surprise and might occasion some excitement to discover that there are material objects, in the sense just noticed. Imagine, for this purpose, a small company of ghosts on a first visit to hard reality. Ghosts, of course, are well acquainted with space, but not with material objects. And now, for the first time, they observe human beings. They observe that human beings when they come to a tree walk around it. Human beings do not walk through walls. They climb over them. Human beings when they meet, step aside and pass. Ghosts, on the other hand, mingle their substance freely. They pass right through one another, like two plumes of smoke, but they are not scattered. "Odd," said one ghost, "None of these things are in the same place with another." "That's right," said another. "They seem to be limited to contiguity. That must be a great bother, always having to go around." They noticed that human beings and trees and walls cast shadows, just as Dante once noticed that those damned souls in hell cast no shadows. "Strange," said the tallest ghost, admiring a shadow. "Like us, positively fascinating, but always on the ground." A man passed by carrying a sack of potatoes, grunting, his back bent under his load. He walked right through one of the ghosts, expecting the ghost to step aside. He blinked and the ghost smiled. They noticed a child bouncing a ball against a wall and saw another child bump his head and run home crying with his feet on the ground, not skimming. The bouncing ball was a wonder to them.

When the ghosts got home they made their report to all the inhabitants of ghost town, and they had one of their writers, one who writes for others, keep the record. And for a long time these ghosts talked about the unghost objects which they had seen.

If now Moore had said that "almost everybody" and, perhaps, even a few ghosts, believe that there are such things as trees, walls, human beings, potatoes, rubber balls, and that among human beings these are called material objects and among some ghosts these are perhaps called unghost objects, then there would have been no difficulty about this. Anyone who has tried to walk through somebody or who has carried a sack of potatoes or bounced a ball or even held a bottle, would recognize immediately what he was talking about. But, in this case, nothing is hidden and there seems no occasion for any human being, at least, to claim that he has discovered such things. A ghost, as we have seen, might do so, but this involves special circumstances.

In what sense, then, are we to understand "material objects" in the required way that they be both hidden and discovered? It is obvious that this conception is relative to that of sense-data. We may understand this in terms of Moore's question: "What exactly is it that happens when (as we should say) we see a material object?" We know what happens. A sense-datum intervenes. The eye is represented, in this situation, as having something like a mysterious catalytic influence upon, let us say, an envelope, so that when the eye is turned upon it, the envelope emits something analogous to a smoke screen or better, camouflage, a camouflage so well adapted to deception, were this the purpose, that most people never do catch on. In any case the "material object" due to what happens whenever we do perceive a "material object" is completely covered, hidden, in the dark. Under these circumstances what is really amazing is that we should be aware that sense-data are hiding something. In this context Moore uses such expressions as "an obscure belief," "believe, however, obscurely," "in this obscure way," which expressions show how hard it is to conceive of man getting a glimpse of what lies behind the sense-datum.

And now what about the clue? What has led to the discovery of what is hidden? We have already noticed the clue which leads to the discovery of sense-data, namely, such a sentence as "The envelope looks like a rhombus," and now as the incidence of the expression "material object" is intertwined with that of the expression "sense-data" so the sentence "The envelope is rectangular" is intertwined with the sentence "The envelope looks like a rhombus." As now the latter sentence, regarded in a certain way, has led to the discovery of sense-data, so the former sentence, regarded in a certain way, as contrasted with the looks-like sentence, leads to the discovery of something in the dark which has no looks at all. The situation is somewhat as follows: If you put on the policeman's clothes, then, of course you look like a policeman. But suppose I want to know who you really are. Then you put on a sailor's clothes, and so you look like a sailor. But, of course, you are neither policeman nor sailor. I complain and you try on other suits of clothes. Finally you appear before me naked, and I am still not satisfied. I say, "That won't do. Those are the emperor's new clothes and you're not the emperor." Or I say, "Remove your skin. You can't fool me that way." However you appear before me, I complain that I want to see *you*, and complain too that you are hiding from me. Your nonappearance is most phenomenal.

Is now the excitement of the philosopher in this case also intelligible? Well, suppose that you, at a certain stage in your philosophical development, unmindful of Descartes' instructions to get your feet well-planted somewhere before you set out, were now convinced that wherever you looked and whatever you heard, wherever and whatever were sense-data. You might, of course, have tried to turn the edge of a sense-datum, but in that case, there would only be another sense-datum. This would be like living in a dream. This would be frightening. And now imagine that in the midst of this dream you open your eyes, and look about you into the darkness, and find yourself believing "however, obscurely," but most certainly, that there are material objects; would not that be a great relief? Well, this might be what the discovery of "material objects" is like. Of course, the philosopher does not discover this by anything like waking from a dream. The clue does not consist in the perceived darkness into which one peers between dreams. It consists rather in a peculiarity of sentences of a certain kind. I have tried to indicate what that is.

I have noticed now two cases of the hidden and the nature of the clue in each case. The first is that of sense-data, and the clue in such a sentence as "The envelope looks like a rhombus." The second is that of the "material object," and the clue is such a sentence as "The envelope is rectangular." I have also tried to indicate what it is that makes of such sentences clues. They must be taken in a certain way, interpreted, that is, in terms of the use of certain other sentences which are like them. In this way such sentences serve as chinks through which, as it were, one peers into the darkness, fascinated by the flickerings in that darkness, lights which enter through the chink one peers through, and from that side.

Now I should like to consider "universals." Universals are also among "the most important kinds of things in the universe." And are universals also hidden? Of course. Most people have never heard of them. And many people who are told about them and who are directed to discover them, never do discover them. Those, relatively few, who have discovered them have, however, established a definite technique for their discernment, and it is to this technique that we must attend in order to understand this discovery. In this case we begin, however, not with sentences, but with certain individual words. Words are the clue, and what, of course, is involved here is that they, words, have meaning. A word, it must be remembered, is usually, in a certain aspect, either a noise or a trail of ink. And yet such noises and such trails of ink have about them an atmosphere of mystery, almost as though they bore within them secret recesses of treasure and power. They are charmed noises, charmed trails of ink, which lead a borrowed life. They are like iron filings which dance and shimmy, at the behest of a magnet hidden, removed, invisible. Noises and trails of ink are alive, but the source of their life is not within them. It lies, of course, in their meanings. I should like to emphasize this point. Considering that words are mere noises and mere ink trails on a white surface, is not their behavior amazing? Is it not clear that something else moves them? They are not self-moving, not animals.

The question is: What moves them? Consider, as Moore does, the word "two." This word, in all its variations in all languages, has been in the world a long time, and there has been, to use an expression of Moore's, "an enormous number" of charmed occurrences of this noise, and, of course, of charmings. It was so from the beginning. There was the second day, one, two. "And God made two greats lights." "And the name of the second river is Gihon," one, two. And some years later: "And of every living thing of all flesh, two of every sort, shalt thou bring into the ark." Two has a long history. And the meaning of "two" has been exercising its influence upon noises and trails of ink for a long, long, time. One thing is clear, and it shows in what I have just noted, and that is, that the meaning of "two," namely two, has played in the background of our times from the beginning. If two is created, it must have been created before most things and perhaps after one. But most people say that two was not created at all. It was before the beginning, that is, before there were any words. Naturally this leaves open the question as to how two enlivens "two." Some people have spoken of "two" as pregnant, and as wedded to two, that is, to its meaning. Some people have spoken of words as inspired, and that suggests two breathing the essence of its substance into "two." But some others who are less given to speculation say that the influence is electric and have their hopes set on advances in electronic studies for catching quiddity on a wire.

The point of what I have just written is to bring out that the meaning of "two" is conceived as a thing, and this thing is intended or looked upon as explaining this remarkable difference between noises which are meaningless and those which have meaning. I want now to introduce a more sober figure which may once more show how the analogy through which one attempts to understand meaning leads to the conception of meaning as something hidden. Think of the word "two" as bearing in the belly of its "o" an arrow pointed in any direction you please. It bears such an arrow in every one of its billions of occurrences. Obviously, these billions of arrows point in all directions. Now, a word, in effect, directs you to its meaning as an arrow directs you to the town. So the meaning is something such that if you pursue the direction in which the arrow in the belly of the "o" points, you will come upon the meaning of the word. But now we meet this puzzling situation. The meaning of "two" in these billion occurrences is the same in all. Moore stresses this point in the following phrases, "identical," "identically the same," "same," "identically same." The arrow, accordingly, in the belly of any "o" of any "two," points at the same two, that is, the same meaning as does the arrow in the belly of any other "o" of any other "two," rain or shine. But how can a billion arrows pointing in all directions all point at the same, identically same, thing? The answer is that this is just the sort of thing that two is.

I have introduced these analogies in order to show how in terms of them meaning may be revealed as something hidden. In relation to the quivering word, the meaning may be the dis-apparent father. In relation to the word with a referent, the referent is the village over the hill. In any case the meaning is regarded, as some people would say, as transcendental, over the hill and far away. And now I should like to notice the clue. Consider, as an ideal of explanation, the following. If someone asks, "Who is Elizabeth?" then, if Elizabeth is in sight, and you, looking at Elizabeth, say, "That is Elizabeth," this explanation should be effective. It is simple and easy to understand. There is the name "Elizabeth" and there is Elizabeth and you, with your look and the formula "That is Elizabeth," make the connection, lay the name on Elizabeth. All this happens in daylight and Elizabeth is in sight. Now consider: What is two? That is, what is "two" the name of? If, now, two stood in the garden and it was daylight, see how simple this would be. You would look at two and say, "That is two." But two is not standing in the garden. If in this situation you ask the question "What is two?" so that it now seems, at any rate, that you do not know, then though you may at the same time have a vague familiarity with two, still, as contrasted with Elizabeth, two is certainly hidden. And on the other hand, if in this situation you are asked the question "What is two?" and it now seems to you that you certainly do know what two is, then, though you may at the same time suffer from baffling unfamiliarity with two, in any case, as contrasted with Elizabeth, two is certainly hidden. In any case, two is hidden. But at the same time two is; for otherwise, how should we speak of two bananas, two rivers, two days, two mosquitoes?

Now what precisely is the clue? The clue is such a question as "What is two?" but it is a clue only as seen through such another question as "Who is Elizabeth?" (or "What is a chair?"). There is a form of explanation which goes with "Who is Elizabeth?" which one now seeks to follow also in explaining "What is two?" The bafflement which one meets in this attempt is explained by the hiddenness of two. Two is certainly a baffling kind of Elizabeth.

And now can you understand a philosopher's excitement about this? It is true, certainly, that there is nothing disquieting about this, as there might very well be in the discovery that there are sense-data. Nor again is there anything reassuring about this, as one's disquiet about sense-data has already been relieved by the discovery of "material objects." But there is other excitement. Columbus discovered a new world, and certainly that was exciting. And so it is with universals, "the world of universals," otherwise hidden in the careless ignorance of people who do not notice that a word's having meaning is like an arrow pointing to the village over the hill. Imagine someone, for the first time, discovering the sky full of stars. For universals, too, are "as the sand which is upon the sea shore." The discovery of universals has stirred the imagination as no other discovery in philosophy has ever done. Silver statuettes shining like stars!

In these pages I have tried to understand Moore's philosopher. I have tried to do this hoping to see what that "most important and interesting thing" is "which philosophers have tried to do." I wanted especially to see how it was "important and interesting," in order to explain some of the excitement that goes into the writing of such a book as this. In order to do this I employed the figures of Robinson Crusoe and Gulliver. They, too, described, mentioning all sorts of most important kinds of things which they had seen. This helped me to see both how what Moore did was like what they did, and also how what he did was different from what they did. They were all discoverers, and they all wrote home about what they had discovered. There were "melons and grapes" and "sense-data," and "material objects" and a "huge creature," and "pleasant savannahs and meadows" and "universals." The difference between these different sorts of things immediately suggests different means of discovery. Robinson Crusoe and Gulliver sailed, landed, and looked. But Moore stayed at home. So the question which I attempted also to answer was: How did Moore come upon the discovery of these things? Naturally I have given only a sketch of what, I take it, furnished Moore with means of discovery. It seemed to me, then, that just as there are chinks in walls and fences along which we pass each day and which chinks we miss seeing at all unless we look from a certain angle, so too there are chinks in the world, sentences, which when we look at them curiously from a certain angle, open out upon "most important kinds of things." I have tried to indicate what some of those chinks are.

In the writing of this paper I have been led especially to notice the ideas clustered about the idea of discovery, namely, the ideas of the hidden and the clue. In this way I came upon the idea of chinks. Among philosophers who have written during the last fifty years, there is none in whose writings the chinks are more clearly identified than they are in the writings of Moore. Moore has always found light by close scrutiny of phrases and sentences. And in telling us of what he saw, he has always respected fastidiously the confines of the chink. It may well be that Moore has in this way brought out into the open what philosophers have always tried to do, generally, of course, with more abandon, without Moore's severity, stretching the chink. All this has been very important in preparation for the question: But are phrases and sentences chinks? We can be grateful to Moore for our re-examination of this conception which, as I take it, Moore has employed with such uncommon skill and patience.

"ON MANY OCCASIONS I HAVE IN SLEEP BEEN DECEIVED"*

I WANT IN THIS PAPER to discuss a fragment of a sentence from Descartes. We are all acquainted with the context of the sentence, since the argument into which it enters is the ever-popular argument concerning dreams. The fragment is the hinge upon which the argument turns. The fragment is: ". . . on many occasions I have in sleep been deceived . . . ." This comes to: In dreams we are deceived.

We might now consider this sentence under the heading: Is it so? and what makes Descartes or anyone else think that it is so? This is direct and looks simple. It is not, and, as is usually the case in studying what any philosopher says, we shall need to ask: What does he mean? So let us turn to this first.

What, then, does Descartes mean when he says: "On many occasions I have in sleep been deceived. . ."? And now I can imagine someone remarking: "What's all the mystery? You know what it is to be deceived and you know what it is to sleep and you know what it is to be in sleep, and so that's it. You are deceived in sleep." This makes it seem as simple as: On many occasions I have in Chicago been deceived or murdered, or something like that. There is nothing strange about that. And

* Presidential address delivered before the fifty-fifth annual meeting of the Western Division of the American Philosophical Association at the University of Chicago, May 2, 3, 4, 1957.

what might happen in Chicago might happen in sleep or anywhere else. You run all these syllables together, and everything
comes out all right. This is, I think, a valuable suggestion, and
is succinct and neat. All the same, this frightens me. Let me ask:
But what is it like to be deceived in Chicago? You meet someone on State Street. You are new in the city. He tells you a hard
luck story. His wife ran off with all his money and his children,
and now he has no money to support them. Would you lend him
a goodly sum just to tide the family over? He will pay you again
as soon as he can arrange a loan with a loan company which he
owns. You are bulging with money and you give him a goodly
sum. The next day you meet the man attending sessions of the
American Philosophical Association. You both laugh, and you
think it's a big joke. He buys you a dinner with your money.
He's a generous, good-natured philosopher. Visiting the pier in
Chicago, you go to see the big boats. While you are watching,
suddenly you see a woman, having leaped from somewhere into
the cold water. Poor unfortunate! Forlorn love, perhaps.
Deserted by some scoundrel. There is no one to help. You
throw aside your coat, leap onto the railing of the pier where you
are standing, and swim out to the struggling woman. You expect
a fight. She will resist your rescue. You are a good swimmer. As
you approach her, she seems suddenly quiet, relaxed, as though
she were out for a float. You halloo to her and seize her by the
collar of her dress. And, then? Why, the woman you would have
saved is a mannikin out of a store window, done up in frills and
fancies. You drop your burden, swim back to the pier, clamber
up to where you were, and there you are greeted with "Bravos!"
from six boys. You throw six boys into the water. On another
occasion you ask someone how a certain machine works, and
he gives you a completely bogus account. Other people ask, and
now you tell them the bogus account you heard. A week later
someone else tells you how the machine works.

As you can see in these cases being deceived isn't what anyone goes in for. Apart from the loss of money, and the wet
clothes on the pier and your complete loss of confidence in your

judgment concerning what someone says concerning how a machine works, the fact is that in all these cases you were deceived. No one wants to be deceived. It's humiliating. Are you going to tell your friends about the man who got your money, about the doll you saved from the whale, about your lectures on how the machine runs? They will laugh at you. You'd better keep your naive soul under wraps and be a chump in private. And after this, stay home. What now, then, goes with being deceived? Sheepishness, apologies, "Of course, I should have known better," and resolution not to let it happen again, "Next time I'll be on my guard."

Now, let us consider what it would be like to treat dreams as cases of deception. So someone tells you with a sad face, remorseful, or at least, regretful, in what it was he was deceived. He may blame himself or he may blame his fate. "How was I to know it was only a doll?" "How was I to know I wasn't King?" It's a grim business. He may react with bitterness. "Every night I go to bed there's the same prospect. I'll be bamboozled again. And every morning I wake again exasperated." He did his best, but his best was of no avail. It isn't fair! The injustice of it! For notice that dreams come just when a man is least able to defend himself, when he is as helpless as a log, fast asleep. One might as honorably steal blankets and bottles from a baby's crib. It's worse than doing a man dirt behind his back. At least, such a man may turn. And what is worse, there is no hope that in the future one may escape. One may stay away from Chicago. One may talk back to tellers of hard-luck stories. One may also get one's revenge, throwing six boys into the deep. But there's no staying away from dreams. They are unavoidable. A man must sleep or die. And there is no such thing as learning to cope with dreams. They always get the best of one. "The lot of man is not a happy one." If a man is to walk through this life by day with trepidation, wary, full of guile, think of his state when going to sleep. One thing is sure, he will be taken in. And he cannot even choose how. Afterwards there's only the memory of this humiliation. Also, one never does find out just how the deception is worked. There are no sleeves to search, no hats to ransack. One doesn't even know where to look. If there is a magician in the place, he is gone by the time one discovers there was one.

And in case now this should be the proper reaction of a man to his dreaming, what should our behavior be, we who listen to one who tells his dreams? Is it not to weep? For notice the man comes to confess. Original sin. I dreamed last night. I was deceived. Or he comes to lament. Original defect. Original predicament. In either case, how are we to react? His shame is our shame. His defect is our defect. Proud man, who aspires to truth and big talk by day, is every night brought low, to his high-mind's undoing. So how are we to speak, to act, when someone tells his dream? Are we to say: "Well, that's your funeral?" For shame! His funeral is our funeral. "The bell it tolls for thee." You, too, dream. So, then, hear his lamentation. Remember: No one likes to be deceived—at least, no self-respecting man or ostrich does. There is no sand to bliss your ignorance. There was a popular song some years ago entitled: "Don't tell me what you dreamed last night; I've been reading Freud." And now we have something similar: "Don't tell me that you dreamed last night; I've been reading Descartes." Freud, of course, is interested in *what* you dreamed last night, and Descartes chiefly in *that* you dreamed last night. Is there not embarrassment in either case? I have, in any case, been startled to discover how much of a parallel one could, for a certain purpose, construct in this case.

And now notice that if, as was said above, we are to understand the fragment of Descartes' sentence on the model of "on many occasions I have in Chicago been deceived," then it appears that Descartes' sentence must come to most people as a surprise and news. And furthermore even on those who are inclined to say what Descartes says, it seems not to make any impression. They go on telling their dreams as nonchalantly as they always have, and they are not in the least ashamed. Have these people then no conscience that they publish what should be their shame, so lightly? People do not usually go about telling their exploits as dupes. Isn't it odd then that a man should take this relish in his own deception or in telling his dreams? And that others should relish it, too? Is deception any the less deception because deception is so common? There are, of course some people who shy away from telling their dreams. ("Has this man no feeling of his business, that he sings at grave-making?") But these people shy away from telling their dreams, not because they don't like to admit to being deceived, but, on the contrary, because they cannot stand the truth, and cannot stand other people's enduring what they themselves cannot stand, the truth. The truth is something scandalous, and dreams are supposed to shout it loud to those who have that particular sort of trained ears. It seems, accordingly, that some people say: "Dreams lie." Other people say: "Dreams never lie."

It has been suggested [1] that dreaming might be thought of as a form of practical joke, or kidding, and that if one took a dream in this way and the joke didn't go too far, no legs broken, just a plain case of falling off one's chair, or wiping a smudge off one's face, then, of course, one would take the dream like a good sport and join in the fun. And, then, of course, there would be no occasion for this humiliation and commiseration. In this case someone would tell his dream and everyone would understand that the teller of the dream was telling about a practical joke played on him while he slept. He would set the table on a roar. And, then, someone would ask: "And who do you think did it? Who was the kidder who kidded you?" After all, a practical joke without the joker, or kidding without the kidder, is bare. There would be little relish in that. And, then, of course, he would tell who it was or whom he suspected. And, then, there would be more laughter. And who, then, was it? It might be anyone, but where one has no reason for suspecting anyone, and one has no practical-joking friend, well, there's always Queen Mab. Who

[1] I am gratefully indebted for this suggestion both to Shakespeare and to Professor Paul Henle. But neither Shakespeare nor Henle is to be held responsible—at least, not very much—for what I say.

did it, then? "Queen Mab, the galloping imp. If I catch her, I'll tickle her antenna." Is this, then, how we are to understand Descartes? Does Descartes think that when he dreamed, Queen Mab, or some other spinner, put on a show for him, pretending to him it was his very self sitting before the fire, etc.? There is no trace of this, either. Descartes is neither humiliated by the deception nor does he regard it as sport. Descartes is plainly puzzled.

"On many occasions I have in sleep been deceived." This sentence may also bring back scenes of childhood. In at least fifty-one homes in Chicago this morning some young mother has found her little boy hiding under the blankets. "Why, Peter, why are you hiding?" And little Peter says, whimpering, "I don't want the bear to get me." And, of course, the bear doesn't get Peter. Bears won't touch anything under blankets. Then his mother says: "There isn't any bear. You've been dreaming." And almost certainly that is the case. Perhaps something like this happens a number of times. Some morning he gets up in a hurry to look for Jimmy in the garden behind a bush. They've been playing hide-and-seek. But Jimmy isn't there. And Peter comes into the house quite disappointed. So his mother comforts him again. "You dreamed it, honey. Jimmy isn't in the garden." By the time he's three Peter has caught on. He doesn't hide under the covers anymore, and he doesn't rush out of sleep into the garden to look for Jimmy. Now, there may be some older people who are like Peter. Once or twice a year, early in the morning, they find this man, up in a tree, quite distressed, and in his pajamas, all rumpled. He too is hiding from the bear. Now one might say about Peter and about this man that they have in sleep been deceived. Peter's mother didn't put it this way. She said: "There isn't any bear, honey. You've been dreaming." We might also say that they have not learned the meaning of "I dreamed." Once they catch on to that, they no longer hide. And they wouldn't even dream of saying: "I was deceived."

It is possible then that Descartes meant something like: "On many occasions I have in sleep been deceived" and on waking, hid from a bear? Not at all possible. And now I want to say that that man who said, "Well, you know what it is to be deceived and you know what 'in sleep' is, and so on, and so you should understand Descartes' sentence," doesn't help us to understand. For they say that they dream, and that they are deceived in dreams, and yet do not show the least shame or regret, or react as they might to kidding or to a practical joke. And what sort of deception is this that a man has no regard for, that doesn't affect him at all? These are, after all, sensitive souls, who would normally be offended at a lie. But they tell their dreams with zest. "Last night I was deceived, in my sleep." "Oh, I much more." "Very interesting. Very interesting!" "Very vivid flim-flam." A dirty trick, I say. In any case I should like now to approach this sentence from a slightly different angle.

Let us ask: Just how did Descartes come to say this? Can we figure out how he found this out? I think we all know that the Positivists, under the embarrassments of some misunderstanding, have reminded us that we can sometimes get a perspective of the meaning of an expression, a sentence, or at least some part of the meaning, if we pursue questions of this sort. So, perhaps, we may in this way also get some clue as to what this sentence means. How then did Descartes discover that in dreams we are deceived? I want in the first place to set aside a suggestion which comes from some of our distinguished members who say that some other nameless people say that Descartes got what he says from ordinary language, that is, from what a lot of other nameless, ordinary people say. In this case, then, someone would ask Descartes: Why do you say that? and he would reply, "If you take note of what people say when they tell their dreams, at breakfast, for instance, you will discover—it was a surprise to me, too!—that some people in telling their dreams begin: Last night I dreamed—..., and others begin: Last night I was deceived in my sleep. These expressions are used interchangeably and the same people use both expressions, now one, now the other. So my sentence comes to: 'I dreamed . . . ,' means the same as: 'In sleep I was deceived.'" He might add, of course, that this is of no significance whatsoever. If this interchangeability strikes you as odd, this may be because you are used to speaking German, and in German there is no such equivalence. Let me insist that were there such equivalence, this would not be of the slightest significance, of no more significance than: Some people say "I dreamed . . . ," all the bassos say this in a low voice, and some other people say "I dreamed," all the sopranos say this in a high voice, and "I dreamed" means "I dreamed," high voice or low voice. But did Descartes get his sentence, then, in this way? Of course not. There isn't a trace of this in ordinary language. And if these nameless ones, ordinaries, said anything like this, may they live to see better days. Of course, it is possible that they said something which looks or sounds a little like this, and there may have been some misunderstanding concerning just what they said. In any case this won't help to understand Descartes.

And, now, since we have considered the suggestion that Descartes came to say what he said by way of noticing what Tom, Dick, and Harry and their triplet sisters say, someone else may suggest that Descartes came to say what he said by way of noticing what extraordinary people say, speaking extraordinary language. But since Descartes is himself chief among such extraordinary people, and since, in any case, that extraordinary people do or do not say those extraordinary things would be of no significance in trying to understand them, then we'll not pursue this suggestion, either.

Before I go on to consider some other possibility, I'd like to take another look at Descartes' sentence. Let's take the sentence: In dreams we are deceived. I want particularly to notice the word "dream." Suppose someone tells his dream. He says: "Last night I dreamed I was Icarus [2] and drove the sun-chariot

[2] Someone has reminded me that it was Phaeton and not Icarus who drove the sun-chariot. But since this is a dream, I am allowing Icarus to have his way about this.

through the sky." (He had been reading about rocket-ships.) His brother says: "Well, that was an interesting dream." Someone comes in and asks: "What was an interesting dream?" and his brother says: "He dreamed last night that he was Icarus and drove the sun-chariot through the sky." My question is: When a man tells his dream, is what he tells his dream, or is it conceivable, for instance, that a man should tell his dream and that he should get it wrong? Is there something else which is his dream, and which he merely reports and concerning which he now may make mistakes? Consider. They say that there are some people who never dream. How they understand what it is they do not do, I don't know. Perhaps all there is to it is that they never tell dreams, though it must sometimes also strike them as strange that other people do. In any case, one could understand how they might compete at breakfast and make up stories which they would introduce as dreams, "Last night I dreamed . . . ." Someone might ask: "Did you really dream that?"

"Of course, can't you hear me?"

"But dreaming isn't telling dreams."

"What, then?"

And, then, the bonafide dreamer is stumped. He says, "We dream, of course." After a pause, he goes on. "There are goings-on in the night."

"Where?"

"In our sleep."

"In your sleep? Where's that?"

And now the dreamer has nothing to show for all his trouble. He has no more to show than does the person who makes up a story. Now my question can be put in this way: Is Descartes saying something about the goings-on in the night or is he saying something about what the teller of dreams tells? Is a dream what a man says it is, and in this respect like the Constitution, which is what the supreme court says it is? Is Descartes saying that there is something deceptive about the goings-on in the night in the way in which there is something deceptive about the goings-on on the stage when a magician puts on a show? The woman isn't actually sawed in two. It only appears to be so. So, too, you didn't actually drive the sun-chariot. You only seemed to drive the sun-chariot. And is it now as by a kind of review of the dream, the goings-on, that he discovers that there was a deception, just as after the magic show he may figure out just how it was the magician waved his scarf to flutter your attention? My impression is that this is certainly how Descartes thinks of dreams. He runs into trouble, then, precisely because in looking back upon the dream he can discover nothing which gives the goings-on away (they are not what they seem) in the way in which he can discover what gives the goings-on away in the case of the magician.

What I have now written, I have written to give some explanation of why it won't do to explain Descartes' saying what he said merely by noticing, in the way described, what people say. Did he then try, as I have suggested, to review his dreams, the goings-on, and so discover that in dreams we are deceived? Let's suppose he tried. But might he not in that case have discovered that in the case of some dreams at least men are not deceived, and would it not then have been accidental that he, Descartes, was always deceived? Consider. King Pharaoh believed in dreams. He dreamed and believed in his dream, but he could not make out what the dream said. It was a dream about seven lean kine and seven fat kine. There was also Joseph, an accomplished dreamer, and a believer in dreams and an interpreter of dreams. Dreams are in this respect very much like foreign languages. There is also in the scriptures a prophet who interpreted dreams and on one occasion told the King, the King being much disturbed by a dream which he could not remember, what the King had dreamed. All this need not strike us as very remarkable in 1957. There are many of the Joseph brotherhood today who also interpret dreams. Their maxim is: Dreams never lie. Of course, interpreters may misinterpret, but this is because the language in which dreams are written is very difficult. It seems in any case that Pharaoh, in the dream cited, and by way of the interpreter got a long range weather forecast, seven years of plenty and then seven years of drought. And now if later someone had asked King Pharaoh whether he was deceived in dreams, he would certainly have replied: "Perhaps. But there was one dream which told me true. In it I was not deceived. Everything came out just as the dream said." Of course, there might be other dreams of which he might have said: "We never made out that one." And of another he might have said: "That dream lied. The interpretation was correct, unmistakable. But the grasshoppers never did come." In those days dreams commonly forecast the future. In our day they forecast nothing but the past. My point now in introducing this consideration is that in this instance we have a context, a way of taking dreams, in which Descartes' language has an intelligible employment. Are we deceived in dreams? Sometimes. Some people say: Never. That Descartes has nothing of this sort in mind is clear from this that he says that we are always deceived in dreams. And if we are always deceived in dreams, then interpretation is meaningless. It is only by way of dreams whose meaning is unmistakable, and which come true, that one is provided with a key. Clearly Descartes did not take dreams in this way. But how, then, did he take them?

There is another interesting expression in the scriptures— namely, "And there appeared to him in a dream . . ." —and then there follows some message, an order or a warning of some sort. No doubt there are people in all times who understand certain dreams in this way. "My mother came to me in a dream last night. . . ." Now here again there would be occasion for the use of the expression: "On many occasions I have in sleep been deceived" or "not been deceived," and then one could go on to say "by my mother," "by a blonde angel," "by a parrot," etc. In any case, this too will not do. Descartes is not thinking of any special dreams. It is true, of course, that Descartes once dreamed a dream which he, himself, interpreted as warning him about his past life and as directing him to pursue the vocation which he later followed. In this connection Descartes employs the words "revelation" and "spirit of truth." Descartes also writes that "the genius that had heightened in him the enthusiasm which had been burning in him for the past several days had forecast these dreams to him before he had retired to his bed." It seems in any case that Descartes might have written of this dream in this way: On at least one occasion I have in sleep been led into the truth. I am not saying that this is in any way inconsistent with: In dreams we are deceived, since we have not as yet managed to tie any meaning to this. It still looks strange.

Up to this point I have been busy trying to show that there is something peculiar about Descartes' sentence. I pointed out that if, for instance, a man says that he was deceived last night, meaning that he dreamed last night, he shows no embarrassment about this and no resentment. How can he be so cheerful about this? Does he think that somehow, like Descartes in the sixth meditation, he will laugh last, when, that is, God gives him the signal? I may add that neither is it a recommendation. To Descartes it must have seemed more like the discovery of something quite familiar. Then I went on to say that Descartes' sentence certainly is not a grammatical one, intended to describe how we use certain expressions, interchangeably, that is. And last I set up for comparison such a use of Descartes' sentence as Pharaoh and other readers of dreams make and whatever it is that Descartes has done.

Now I should like to return to the first question I introduced at the beginning of this essay. The question is: Is it so?—that is, is it so that we are deceived in dreams? And my answer is: It is neither so nor not so. Either answer is based on a misunderstanding. Are berries right or wrong? How would you answer that—yes or no? It is true, of course, that the question I asked does not look at all, nor strike one at all, as like this one about berries. No one could take the latter seriously. Nevertheless, I want to suggest that however serious one may be in dealing with my question, which is also Descartes' question, one will not get out of the woods until one also comes to see that it is also *like* the question about berries. The latter is, of course, a deliberate misdemeanor, if, that is, it can be said to be demeanor at all. There is nothing deliberate about Descartes' question, and, of course, it is much more important than a misdemeanor. Now, then, I want to explain this.

It may be noted that Descartes does not explain his sentence. He gives no reasons. It must, then, have seemed to him to require no reasons. It may even now seem strange that his sentence should be brought to this sort of question. Doesn't everybody know that in dreams we are deceived? Whatever explanation is given of Descartes' sentence must also explain this that it is difficult even to bring it into question. I should like then to suggest that Descartes never did discover this, that he never did deliberately make it up as though he were saying some new thing, and, also, he never figured it out. Even when it led him into such difficulties, he never questioned it. What then? Well, it's rather as though he were stricken with this sentence—struck by it as with something with which he is as familiar and at home as he is with his hands and feet. It is native to him in his language, and so too the matter of resistance never comes up. One doesn't resist one's hands and feet. The sentence has by insinuation, on the sly, made its way. But how then? By way of an allurement, a seduction, a charm, a compulsion, a sorcery. And what now exercises these strange powers? The evil genius? I do not think so. In any case I mean to say that Descartes, like all the rest of us, is lured, seduced, charmed, compelled by an analogy, an analogy of a special sort, an analogy which keeps one's mind in a certain fixed position, and of which he is himself unaware. And this is how it comes about that Descartes says that in dreams we are deceived.

It has been said that seeing through an analogy is like seeing through spectacles. Imagine, then, that you are seeing through spectacles on the lenses of which designs are drawn. Imagine now, further, that when you look at designs on a paper, you see the lines which are part of the design on the lenses of your spectacles as part of the design on the paper. This will, obviously, result in some confusion, and until you become aware of the design on the lenses of your spectacles, you will not see clearly the design on the paper. You must remove those spectacles. The analogy to which I have referred plays a part like that of the design on the lenses of your spectacles. The analogy, it must be remembered, is not out in the open. It is nothing Descartes speaks of. ("Even your best friends [I, for instance] won't tell you.") It is submerged, underground. It is, accordingly, like a design on the lenses of one's spectacles of which one is completely unaware. No wonder, then, that one sees in a confused way the design on the paper.

Before I go on now I should like to raise this caution. The explanation I will give touches the fringes only of an account of all language and of philosophy, of such magnificence and depth, that I am unceasingly amazed that any mere human being should ever have come upon it. And now my caution. If we compare the account to which I have referred, to some gorgeous tapestry, an intellectual design of Bayeux proportions and needle-fine, then my sketch of an explanation of the fragment from Descartes must be compared to some tiny segment, cut out of the splendid frame, and now pale and tattered and a sorry thing. I have the heart to present it only as it now gives me occasion to tell you where I got it. I wish that my essay might for this purpose have more push. And now this further. I will present the sketch of an explanation of Descartes' sentence. It is not, however, presented as *the* explanation. The routes by which one may in the mazes of language lose one's way and so find oneself in the confines of some bewildering nowhere are many. Let us say, in the words of Socrates, that one "may venture to think, not improperly or unworthily, that something of the kind is true."

And now I should like to explain the analogy. The analogy is described as "grammatical." In the case of: Are berries right or wrong? there is no grammatical analogy which could explain this. I called it a misdemeanor, but one might call it a crime. Except for the purpose of illustrating crime, or some mischief, it has no excuse. It makes no sense, either philosophical or otherwise. Nevertheless, it bears a certain similarity to "In dreams we are deceived." Remember now that neither of these sentences is here said to be an analogy, though, of course, there may be an analogy between them. The latter sentence, however, bears the traces of an analogy—the grammatical one, that is—and it is this analogy which explains the form of the sentence and our fascination.

What now do I mean by a grammatical analogy?

Consider the following sentences:

Peter tells his dream.

Peter tells a story.

Peter tells what happened.

Here we have on the surface of these sentences obvious similarities. "Peter tells." But there is more than that. If Peter tells, Peter talks; and this will be so, no matter what Peter tells. Furthermore, if Peter tells his dream, Peter remembers his dream. If Peter tells a story, he remembers the story (unless he is making it up). If Peter tells what happened, Peter remembers what happened. Also, if Peter tells, someone listens, even if it is Peter who listens. And what is told is interesting or uninteresting or dull or stupid and so on, in any case. Peter may practice telling. He may be an accomplished teller or again a bungler in telling, and all those may apply in any case. He may in the midst of telling forget what he was to tell. His facial expression, (How did he look when he came to this part? Very grave.), his gestures, (He raised his hand at this point.) and his zest in telling (His eyes shone.), all three are relevant. In connection with his telling you may ask all these sorts of questions, again, no matter what he is telling. This now is what I mean by the grammatical analogy. The sentence forms which go, in this instance, with the first telling, a context, go with the others, too. So one may say: language pattern involved in telling a dream is like that involved in telling what happened. This is right. There are those similarities.

But suppose now that someone went on to say, "And so telling a dream is like telling what happened." Though this may be true, this may also be misleading. For he may now also suppose that all these sentences have the same meaning in these different contexts. Accordingly, he may say remembering is remembering, and whether, then, you remember a dream, or remember a story, or remember what happened, it's all the same. This, of course, is wrong. For notice, in the case of remembering a dream it makes no sense to say: "You got it wrong. That's not how it was." His dream is what he remembers, what he tells. But in case of telling a story or in case of telling what happened, one may certainly remember it wrong. We'll get the book and see. We can check. This is what the book says, and this is what you said. The book says: "Words, words, words, words," and you said, "Buzz, buzz, buzz." And as for what happened, your memory is unreliable. We'll visit the scene, and see, Mr. Falstaff, whether all those dead bodies are still lying on the field. It won't particularly matter in this case whether he is remembering or whether he is lying. What is misleading in such cases is the use of similar expressions or even the same sentences which then tempt us to assume an analogy or sameness in meaning. The point is that the expression may be the same and the meaning different. This is especially tempting when there is generally a wide area both of analogous grammar and analogous meaning. (Who would ever have supposed that the difference between remembering a dream and remembering what happened could be of philosophical significance?) It may be useful also to note that in case Peter tells a story he is making up ("Tell us a story, Uncle Peter"), he remembers nothing at all, and that doesn't mean he is actively forgetting. But it has been suggested that making up stories is a form of discovery, like taking notes on the scene of the happening.

We have noticed the similarity in the grammatical or the sentence pattern of these various bits of discourse, and we have also noticed that beyond this there is also a divergence of pattern. And now I should like to stress a point already made. If someone tells what happened, then, of course, it makes sense to ask such questions as: Are you sure? Did you observe carefully? Were there other witnesses? What do they say?, and to retort with: "You're wrong. That's not how it was." But when it now comes to someone's telling his dream, none of these questions is allowed. And this is not because for some arbitrary reason one doesn't want these questions asked, as though he wanted to hide something, keeping the witnesses of one's dream from testifying. This is a part of the essence of the dream. But certain questions in relation to the telling of a dream are intelligible and certain others which are intelligible in relation to telling what happened are not intelligible in relation to the telling of a dream. In this way one can see both the coincidence and the divergence of these two distinct language patterns.

And now among these several forms of discourse, certainly, that of telling what happened is basic, fundamental. We no doubt learn it first and throughout our lives it is of primary importance. It dominates. The others may be regarded as variations on a theme. One might, then, unwittingly expect that the pattern of it should be repeated in the others. There are now special reasons why there should be this disposition in the case of dreams. In the first place you may tell as your dream, on Monday, what you may tell as what happened, on next Tuesday. This weighed very heavily in Descartes' discussion. Furthermore, you remember your dream and you remember what happened. I have already noticed the misleading character of this parallel. Besides this, in connection with remembering one's dream, one may be visited with vivid imagery, just as one may in remembering what happened. Now, then, I am suggesting that it is the momentum of this grammatical analogy which carries one along the whole way. This is the source of that allurement, that push, that sorcery, which I mentioned earlier.

And so this is how one comes to say that in dreams we are deceived. We can, I think, trace a likely course of this seduction. Thinking in general about what you tell when you tell your dream and what you tell when you tell what happened, you may say, comparing the two, that when you tell your dream, you tell what is not so, what never happened, and when you tell what happened, well, that's what is so. Now this looks like: What you told as your dream is false, and what you told as what happened is true. What is not noticed in this case is that the distinction between what happened and what did not happen, between true and false, falls within the pattern of telling what happened, and is excluded from the pattern of telling one's dream. This shows how easy in language it is to go through an open switch.

Above I used the phrase "thinking in general." It is in this circumstance that one goes through the open switch. The switches are always open. But when one listens to someone telling his dream, one does not go through such open switches. Try this on someone who is telling his dream.

"Ah! So you were deceived?"

"Deceived?"

"Why, yes. Did you not at the time of your dream have the attitude of acceptance? Did you not at the time of your dream believe in your dream, believe in the bear?"

And now what is the teller of dreams to say? Is he to say: "Why, yes, I did have the attitude of acceptance, I did believe in the bear." Where does such language come from? Well, clearly, it comes from the analogy with telling what happened, but not at all in a simple way since the phrases introduced here come, not directly from the context of what happened and of seeing what happened, but from this language as seen through still another analogy. There are cases in which in seeing, one is not sure as to what one is seeing. This, of course, is shown in the language. "I am not sure, but I believe that it's a bear." There are other cases in which one may say, "He believes that it's a bear," or "He's sure it's a bear," when one may oneself be uncertain or may know that there is no bear. One might judge in such a circumstance by the way in which someone else approaches what he takes to be a bear. The phrase "attitude of acceptance" suggests that the question: Shall I accept? has come up and that one has then assumed the attitude of acceptance. (What the heck! One has to take a chance.) This way of looking at perception goes along with the sense-datum theory, such that every time you look at the broad side of a barn something comes between you and the broad-side of a barn (if there is a broad-side of a barn), and you finally make the plunge. After all, they are your cows, and you'd better do some accepting, gambling on the friendliness of sense-data, or of whoever has charge (animal faith) or fret the whole of your milking time away. This is one how, some how, of looking at perception and of telling what happened with which it gets mixed up. Now, then, the point is that if you look at perception in this way (the most ordinary perception involves "acceptance" and "belief"), and if, then, you go on to look at dreams as a form of perception, why then, naturally, you look at dreams, also, as involving "acceptance" and "belief." It turns out, then, to be a case of a lost gamble, misplaced confidence, which you have the further illusion of having uncovered. Descartes' metaphysical embarrassment arises from the fact that he cannot figure out that he ever did uncover this.

Suppose someone said: "No. No, indeed. I wasn't deceived. I saw at once it wasn't a bear. Why, some of the stuffing was showing at the seams. It was a puppet show, that's what it was. And I could see the strings." That he cannot find the stuffed bear or the puppets after he wakes, proves nothing. There are and have been so many stuffed bears and so many puppet shows. What is dreaming but a baffling sort of television? Where did that program come from? It's a big omniverse.

Having said that what is told as one's dream is false, one has also to explain the remembering. How is it possible that I should, at the time of the telling the dream, and so telling what is false, what never happened, how is it possible that I should remember so vividly what never happened? And now what is there to do but draw further on the analogy in which one is already entangled? And so we get the picture of dreaming already referred to above. As you have been a witness to goings-on, of what happened, in case you tell what happens, so too you must have been a witness to goings-on, of what happened in your sleep, in case you tell your dream. That you remember and tell what you now know did not happen, shows plainly that you were deceived. It may help to remind ourselves that people who tell what happened are sometimes mistaken. Suppose now that someone who was a witness to some happening got it all wrong —unaccountably wrong.

Imagine someone who looks out the window which looks out upon a garden with a green lawn and trees and bushes, etc. He looks, and then he rubs his eyes and says: "You know what I saw?" And he tells you about Andromache on the walls of Troy. This would be very odd. He looks out of the window, and he tells what he saw. Perhaps, in such a case, it would do no good at all to take him back to the window. He might see Andromache on the walls of Troy again. One might now think of one's dream in this way. "I looked, and I saw, and lo, and behold!, this is what I saw." He tells his dream. He doesn't remember, however, where it was that he was looking. If one always dreamed, looking out of the window, then, of course, one could always return to the window and make sure that one did not see Andromache on the wall. Since you don't know where you were when in your sleep you were seeing,—who is to say that in such a case you are where you eyes are?—how is one to say that from wherever you were you could not see Andromache on the walls of Troy? Here all the ordinary barriers of perception are done away. So there's no such thing as going back to the window, either to say that Andromache was standing on the wall or that she wasn't. Only if she wasn't, can you say that you were deceived. Descartes has said that he was deceived. But can he show now that he did not see Andromache on the wall, or that he was nowhere in the vicinity, when he in his sleep saw what he saw? He doesn't know what he saw. So, how does he now know that he did not see Andromache on the wall? This is precisely, it—that he doesn't know he didn't, and so he doesn't know he was deceived.

This may help further to show how the analogy with telling what happened befogs one's view of telling one's dream.

I have now also answered my second question: What makes Descartes or anyone else think so? He is under the domination, the influence, of the analogy which I have described. And need I add, and so are all the rest of us? It is not easy to withstand even if one is aware of it. This sentence, then, as we have seen, arises like a bloom out of a confusion, and it serves to gather round its head that cloud, the skepticism of the senses. So, with ridding ourselves of the confusion, we rid ourselves of the sentence, and so also of the problem of skepticism. Eternal vigilance is still the price of keeping in the clear. "And is not that grand!"

And now if there are analogies which mislead, and so confuse, are there not also analogies which may lead us back and help us to see? try this. If you hit a man on the head, he may be stunned and dazed. When he recovers, he says: "OooOh, I saw stars!" Now, then, was he deceived? Would you be interested in showing him that he did not? Are you to say: "No, you didn't. It's mid-afternoon?" Or are you to say that you doubt that he saw stars, and you don't know whether he did or did not? Suppose he offers to hit you on the head so that you can see for yourself. Are you to insist that they are not the same stars we ordinarily see? Suppose he says: "Oooooh, I saw the big dipper." How do you know he didn't? Why isn't a concussion like night? Of course, you may not be at all inclined to say that he was deceived. How much must he say in order for you to say that he was deceived? Suppose you hit him on the head, again, a little harder, and, now, when he recovers, he cries: "Oooh, I saw . . . ," and then he tells you a story. It sounds to you like a dream. I am not now asking at what point you would say he was pretending, but at what point you would say that he was deceived. There is, of course, no question about whether or not he saw stars, anymore than there is a question about whether or not a man dreamed. The question is as to why in the case of a man's dream one is inclined to say that he was deceived, whereas, in the case of a man's seeing stars one is not so inclined. Suppose a man said: "Last night I dreamed I saw stars," and he doesn't mean that he dreamed someone hit him on the head. Was he deceived? Of course, in the latter case in which the man dreamed, he was not hit on the head. Would this, then, show that he was deceived? How? I am not saying that the analogy between "I saw stars" and "I dreamed ..." is complete. I am only suggesting that this analogy may help to lay the spell of the other one.

This reminds me. It is significant that in connection with dreams we ask: What caused him to dream? and sometimes we are satisfied with a sort of explanation. "He ate too much." "He was so excited yesterday at the zoo." "I always dream when I'm low on thyroid." "It was our conversation just before we went to bed." No one explains a dream by saying: "Oh, he wasn't paying attention" or "He was half asleep." The fact is, he was asleep. Nor does one say "He was asleep."

In case of deception, no one says: "He mistook the dry pavement in the sunlight at noon for a wet pavement, or a mirage for an oasis, because, as you know, he ate baked eel at dinner and that always gives him indigestion." Or "Yesterday he was so excited about the monkey at the zoo. Remember how he looked into the monkey's eyes! And today he can't tell a hawk from a hand-saw." One may say: "He was pre-occupied with something—thinking hard about how he would tell his mother and of how he would introduce her to his mother. So he was not attending." Or "But the pavement in sunlight at noon does look like a wet pavement."

Dreams have an explanation in the sense just illustrated. So do deceptions. The difference in the explanation is a difference in the concepts. We explicate the concepts by bringing out these differences. In the case of "I saw stars," the explanation is: "I was hit on the head." And this explanation does not compete with: "They're shooting off fire-works on the beach." In case the former is the explanation, the second is ruled out, whether they are shooting off fire-works on the beach or not.

Of course, there is a maze in the case of dreams. Everybody knows that. The question is: What sort of maze is this?

Consider: Someone says: "It's a horse." Someone else says: "It's a zebra. Horses and zebras are common in this circus." Still another says: "Zebras are horses." So what are you to do? Well, get some horses and get some zebras, and examine them closely. Now, then, are zebras horses? Here now is a similar case. Someone says: "It's a dream." Someone else says: "It's a deception." Still another says: "Dreams are deceptions." So what are you to do? Well, get some dreams and get some deceptions, and examine them closely. Compare. But this is not so easy to do. "Go, and catch a falling star." Go, and catch a dream. Dreams, let me tell you, are not so easy to come by. And deceptions also are hard to get. If, now, you could get hold of a dream and make it stand still ("I saw a dream walking") and could get hold of a deception (Deception stalks) and make it stand still, and if then you could walk around them, doing your subtlest, why, then, you should be able to settle this matter. The problem now reduces itself to a matter of technique. Is there a net for catching dreams and a net for catching deceptions? A dream in one hand, held, hardly a wisp, between your thumb and forefinger, and a deception in the other, held, scarcely a whisper, between your thumb and forefinger—that would be ideal. Butter-fingers!

This analogy, which is also powerful, makes it seem as if the problem concerning dreams were one which is to be settled only by means of further information which remains inaccessible to us. Dreams are more volatile than helium. Dreams explode silently at the mere approach of an enquiring one. In the case of the horses and zebras, presumably, someone finds out more about horses and zebras and in this process there is a refinement of concepts. If horses and zebras invisibled faster than light and disappeared (Pfut!) at the mere shadow of a curiosity about them, why, these scientists would have to give up. Of course, even in such a case, it seems as though horses and zebras are tame enough, so long as no one asks questions. "And thereby," as Shakespeare says, "hangs a tale." For dreams and deceptions, too, are tame enough, so long as no one asks certain questions. I have tried in this paper also to show in what sense one can make a dream and a deception stand still to be examined. One examines concepts—namely, the concepts "dream" and "deception." To do this is to remind oneself of the meanings of these expressions in the patterns of language and circumstance into which they enter. I have not led a dream zebra out, to stand alongside a deception zebra alongside a real zebra, and inspected. I have counted no hairs. With what eye should I inspect? Not with these blue eyes. All the same, I have the urge.

Try to think of the differences in meanings of sentences in terms of the figure of the differences in the branchings of the limbs of trees. There may be similarities in the patterns of such branchings. Two limbs of a tree up to a point show the same branchings off and then may come divergences which are present in one and not in the other. Squirrels commonly have no trouble because of such resemblances and such divergences among branches. They leap and run and frisk. And normally this is also the case with human beings in following routes of language—that is, when they are busy, when, for instance, there are nuts to get. But there are cases in which one takes one's lead in getting perspective of the branchings of one limb of meaning, from the design of the branchings of another, by reason of a dominant similarity. And so one has the illusion that there are divergent branchings when there are none, or none when there are some. The slightest pressure here may give one a strange feeling, a feeling as of suspense between heaven and earth. And this reminds me that philosophy has sometimes been described in this way, as thought in suspense between heaven and earth, one of the children of plenty and of want, a love-child. In any case, if you rest your foot on the absence of the branchings of a limb, on the mere shadow of the branchings of a limb, cast by a similar limb, you may have the illusion of resting securely, up a tree, or you may feel yourself in unstable equilibrium, quite up in the air. But I am not concerned here to speak of squirrels up a tree, or of a man up in the air. I am trying to present a certain way of looking at confusion, the sort of confusion I see in: We are deceived in dreams. Off the limb: Peter-told-his-dream, there is no branch: Peter-was-deceived.

This essay is a clear instance of mitigated plagiarism. My hope is that the plagiarism shows through.

THE BLUE BOOK

WHEN I FIRST BEGAN thinking about writing this paper on The Blue Book, I thought it might be helpful and interesting to find out something about the history of this book. Accordingly I wrote to Miss Alice Ambrose with whose generous permission I am including the following note from her letter in response.

This is the note: "The history of The Blue Book is as follows: Wittgenstein was listed in the Cambridge Reporter as giving two courses of lectures in 1933-34, one being called 'Philosophy for Mathematicians.' To this, as I remember, 30 or 40 people turned up, which distressed him. After three or four weeks of lecturing he turned up at lecture and told the class he couldn't continue to lecture. I remember the occasion and remember how amazed I was that an announced course of lectures could be abandoned in this way. Of the people in that class he chose five of the rest of us to dictate The Blue Book to: H. M. S. Coxeter and R. L. Goodstein, mathematicians, also Francis Skinner (who might have been on a Trinity Grant to do math. though he actually left off doing math. in order to devote himself to Wittgenstein's work), Margaret Masterman Braithwaite and myself. About a month later, I see by a reference to my diary that the five of us had increased to seven, and I know one of them was Mrs. Helen Knight but for the life of me I can't remember the other one. Wittgenstein quarreled with Coxeter because Coxeter quite innocently ran off on a mimeograph the material of the first term's dictation and discussion. So Coxeter didn't continue in the second term. Mrs. Braithwaite also dropped out during the year in the third term. I've forgotten what the unpleasantness was in her case. She and I took down discussion that he wasn't including in The Blue Book and we called this The Yellow Book. He once flew at her for doing so, but as he was also distressed when something he thought good was not taken down because he wasn't dictating—and she pointed this out to him at the time—this practice on our part was allowed to continue. I believe I continued with it after she left. The Blue Book dictation and discussion went on during all three terms along with the other set of lectures—which were evidently attended by quite a large group since I refer to them in my diary as 'big' (12 members I see from one entry). The small group met for The Blue Book each week as regularly as for a class. I can't remember whether this was the year Moore attended his lectures, but I suspect it was. Can't remember how many terms he attended. I have notes from these lectures. But The Blue Book was dictated. I believe I typed some of the dictated material and later on Wittgenstein had it mimeographed —but not a few pages at a time. When he had the material compiled into The Blue Book I don't remember but I suppose after the year was over. Yes, there was discussion during the dictation but what he did at each meeting was not greatly determined by our comments, as I remember it. I believe that what he talked about in the lectures and what he gave us for The Blue Book was pretty different.

"The Brown Book, like The Blue Book, was dictated throughout the three terms along with his regular lecture course. For that Skinner and I were the only ones and we met him 2–4 hours per day, 4 days a week. That was in 1934–35. We sometimes went on beyond term for a few days of the vacation."

In a later note she wrote: "As for your question about how The Blue Book was dictated, as far as I remember he never had even notes with him. I think I remember but once, and I think this was a lecture when he seemed to have a card with him to which he referred once or twice at the beginning of the lecture. It was in general unlike him to write out things ahead. His custom was to dictate, stop for discussion, and continue dictation."

A reviewer is expected to have read and to understand the book he reviews. Accordingly, since I am about to review this book, or something of that sort, naturally I expect that I understand it. And if I understand it, and there are some readers who do not, perhaps I can help them to understand it, or at least help them not to misunderstand in certain ways or help them to misunderstand it in a certain preferred way. This is rather strange since it seems to involve that the author himself failed to help them to understand it or failed to help them enough, and so some reader comes forward to do what the author did not do. In some cases this seems to be how it is. Think of all the helps over hard places for boys and men in reading Kant, for instance, supplied by helpers. Kant couldn't do it. So here are all Kant's little helpers. Very well, then, I too am a little helper. But if I am such a little helper I am going to help myself generously to the helpmost helper, namely, the author himself. I will help the reader to the help offered by the author, reminding the reader of those helps.

This book, notes, discussions, investigations, dictations, contains no introduction, no conclusion, no chapters, no chapter headings, no helpful title. So at the outset there is no guide, no warning, no preparation, no cautionary remark. Perhaps the students to whom these dictations were dictated were better prepared. I doubt it, however. The author may very well have considered and said that a bump is also education, a bump of the right sort, of course—bumping one's head, for instance, against such a question as "What is the meaning of a word?" If accordingly the reader has pretty well absorbed the shock of that question and has gone on reading, since all the words are familiar enough—there are scarcely any strange words,—he may nevertheless soon feel as though he were being turned round and round and then as though this world of words were whirling past him. There seems to be no increment, nothing upon which one can fix his grasp and tell his friends, "This I have found." And if now he tries again, reading more slowly, intent upon this paragraph and then upon the next one, then even though he may seem to understand this paragraph and the next one, he will not understand how they are connected. He may ask himself: And what about that question: What is the meaning of a word? And what have "toves" and the "red flower" of the field to do with it? What is the individuality of a number? How long is a piece of string? And as he pages through the book, the contents may strike him as more and more distressing. Such incoherence! "Bring me a red flower," "We observe certain actions of the amoeba," thinking "performed by the hand," "the visual image two inches behind the bridge of my nose," "Imagine a yellow patch," "Can a machine have tooth-ache?," "Bright's disease," "unconscious tooth-ache," "Do you know the ABC?," "How can we hang a thief who doesn't exist?," "Is your imagination so absolutely exact . . . ?" One may certainly wonder as to how those students learned anything from these dictations and may quit trying oneself. Madness, perhaps, but little method! Of course, one may still go on reading since these pages are studded with scenery, startling and sometimes amusing. So one may go along for the ride.

The impression of incoherence is, I suspect, common to nearly all readers. And there are reasons other than the formal ones I've noticed to account for this. This book is a book in philosophy. And it is read chiefly by readers of philosophy. And with what expectations would such readers read? Obviously they will expect what they are accustomed to getting when they read philosophy. Their disappointment and the measure of incoherence will be determined in the same way. And what are they used to? They are used to proofs, to arguments, to theories, to evidences, refutations, to infallibles, to indubitables, to foundations, to definitions, to analyses, etc. And if in these terms any reader should, having read, seek to turn his reading to some profit and ask himself: What has the author proved, for what has he presented arguments, what is his theory, what has he refuted, and what are his infallibles?, he is certain to be disappointed. The author has neither proved nor refuted anything. And he has presented nothing as infallible, nor a theory. What is such an author doing in philosophy? A skeptic one might admit. He understands the questions and understands what ignorance and knowledge are. He has busied himself about the questions. He has said: "We do not and we cannot know," presumably a respectable answer. The skeptic has tried and failed and investigated the nature of his failure. Man cannot know as he cannot fly. He is not an angel. And this author? This author spends seventy and more pages lolling. He does not, of course, say that he is lolling, which seems anyway obvious enough, since he does it so strenuously, nor that he lolls evading. So he's no angel either. In any case it does strike some readers that this book is the work of a strangely articulate and irresponsible author. He doesn't say "Yes" and he doesn't say "No." The flexible man! Was Descartes right in his statement of the Cogito or not? What we want is an answer: Yes, or: No. And what do we get? Not even a weak answer such as "Probably" or "Not at all likely." Surely a straight-forward question deserves a straight-forward answer. No wonder that man stomped out and slammed the door.

I have been trying in these paragraphs to represent a certain source of misunderstanding, an obstacle to understanding. It may also be represented in this way: Philosophers are people who investigate what sorts of things there are in the universe. They are, of course, scrupulous in these investigations beyond the scrupulosity of any other investigator. They stand at the gate and wait, fearing to tread where angels rush in. And what do they ask? They ask such questions as: Are there angels, universals, pure possibilities, uncrusted possibilities, possibilities with a little mud on them, fairies, creatures made of beautiful smoke, relations, the Lost Atlantis, real equality among toothpicks, sense-data, ghosts, selves in prison with two feet, everlasting shoe-makers, heaven, thinking horses, pure uncontaminated acts, absolutely independent tables, the minds of stars, the spirits of an age, perfect circles, the geometrical point of a joke, the devil, floating impressions, categorical don'ts, one simple called Simon, perspectives waiting to take their places as the penny turns, gods, any ding-dong an sich with a bell so one can find it in the dark, trees, houses, and mountains in the mind, itches of necessary connection, two impossibilities before breakfast, blue ideas, enghosted pieces of furniture, etc.

And if now anyone comes to the reading of this book expecting the author, for instance, to say: "Yes, yes, God exists," and then to show him a new and knock-out proof that is guaranteed for a thousand years or to help him to an old one, long buried in a Kant heap, but now freshly washed and polished, well, the author is more likely to remind him that though Nietzsche some years ago read an obituary notice to the effect that God is dead, he, the author, had not even heard that God was sick. "The living God!" And as for inventing any new apriori synthetic, a new drug to cure this or that, or any and all, sorts of incertitude, though he seems at one time to have been interested in inventing a new type of airplane propeller and showed a keen interest in all sorts of gadgets, a milk bottle, for instance, from which, with the use of a spoon, one could pour off the cream—"Now, there's America for you!"—this particular form of invention he seems not to have been interested in. He was more inclined to recommend a few old home remedies and common herbs, garden variety simples which he was insistent one should not confuse. And as for those readers in general who want answers to their questions and who, if they already have answers, want better reasons, the author gives neither better reasons for the old answers nor any answers, and those readers who keep their questions may be considered either fortunate or unfortunate as the case may be.

I have tried to show how it is that this book should disappoint some readers, supposing that they had expectations in reading it.

I have suggested that the reason why such readers have such expectations is that it is, or is read as, a book in philosophy. And it is a book in philosophy surely? Well, it is and it isn't. It is certainly obvious that the author is busy about philosophical problems. The first sentence in the book is the sentence: "What is the meaning of a word?" and that is a philosophical staple, a sort of thorn which all philosophers carry about with them. And there are others: What is thinking? What is locality? What is a rule? What is expectation? What is time? What is knowledge? So if one were to show someone that this is a book in philosophy and that those readers who were disappointed in it were justified in expecting what they have been led to expect from it, one might point out to him the presence in the book of these questions. Of course, these readers might still be misled. For the question is: Are these questions treated philosophically in the book? and if this means: Are they treated in the way in which such questions are treated by Descartes or Hume or Plato? who either give answers to such questions or at least try to—they certainly are not men of whom one might be tempted to say that they once did good work and then said to themselves, "I have done enough, now I'll rest; let George do it, while I fiddle with words,"—the answer is that they are not treated philosophically. So if some reader complains, "But I thought that the author was another Descartes," we can understand what he was looking for and what led him to this.

And now it would be natural to say that since the author is manifestly aware of these questions, and must know that these questions cry out and have been crying out for centuries for answers, that he does not answer is a bad sign. For either he does not understand these questions and spends his words and his thoughts in evasions, or he understands but cannot answer these questions and now spends his words and thoughts in other evasions. In either case what we seem to have—modesty mercifully tempering judgment—is seventy and more pages of evasion, diversionary tactics, a whole school of red herrings. (Red herrings and straw men and a few dead ducks are most common among the fish, flesh, and fowl in these woods.) It seems in any case that in the midst of these pressing and worrying questions—and what questions could be more urgent? —the author skips about in what strikes some as a kind of philosophical surrealism, juxtaposing the most distantly related ideas such as machines and tooth-aches, and questions and cramps, and mental processes and fidgeting with tea-cups. There are realists, naive realists, sophisticated realists, neo-realists, critical realists, semi-critical realists, and now surrealists. "The cow jumped over the moon."

I have certainly made it plain that the author has not altogether abandoned those questions with which we have been so much occupied. It isn't as though he quite bluntly said that these are not questions, which on the face of it they obviously are—in fact it is precisely the face of it that leads us on. The questions look like questions, sound like questions, and are labored over as questions. There are, in fact, answers too, many answers, and it is said that that there are so many answers shows that the questions are difficult and if askers complain that answerers do not understand answerers this shows it all the more. And now it isn't as though the author said that someone first began trying to find the answers to exclamations and then others joined in and they asked and they answered and did not understand one another's answers and then all talked about what difficult questions the exclamations are. If someone in such a situation had said, "But these aren't questions, they're exclamations," one can imagine the hub-bub that would have ensued. They would have exclaimed and questioned and protested and held up each other's favorite exclamations to show that they were questions and they would have deferred to one another's questions, if not to one another's answers. But this is all foolishness. It isn't at all like that. Still, ...

Whatever these questions are they certainly aren't exclamations. Are they nothing? Well if so they are an especially interesting sort of nothing which can be heard, seen, worried about, respected, etc. We can be sure, too, that these questions are not rhetorical questions, nor pretended questions as though someone made them up to look like and sound like questions. Nor are they to be explained as slips of the tongue or pen, though someone might suggest, jokingly, of course, that when your thinking slips, questions like this might happen. And your thinking slipping is rather like your tongue slipping, an educated tongue, that is. And if, by the way, in this book the word "muddle" should come in it should not be understood that the author intends to *tell* you that these questions are muddles. In what follows I should like to try to explain what he does do.

And now I want to try to help myself to keep a certain perspective of what the author is doing. It may not be the only one nor the most profitable one but it suits me. I say what the author is *doing* rather than what the author is saying in order to prevent the misunderstanding that one could be told what he says and if one then remembered this, that would be what the author aimed at. This would be as though the author aimed to put something in the reader's pocket. But what he does is unlike that. What, then, is he doing? Remember to begin with that these are dictations. They are dictated to a few students. And now I want to say that these dictations are designed in connection with other oral discussions to help in teaching these students an art. Obviously these students must also exercise themselves in practicing this art. "Now you do it." This art has been described in a variety of ways. *It is the art of attacking those questions* we noticed earlier. Attacking is not answering. If this description should give a wrong impression let us say that it is the gentle art of attacking. *It is the art of disentangling.* Disentangling what? Meanings. If it should come as a surprise that meanings can be entangled, be assured, then, that it is a part of the teaching to show how meanings can be entangled and disentangled. *It is the art of cure.* This is, perhaps, the description of the art which is best known. There is physical therapy. There is mental therapy. And here is a specialty. There are mental cramps. Perhaps it will be better to disassociate it from the expression "mental therapy." Let us call it intellectual therapy of a certain sort. *It is the art of finding one's way when lost.* And who is lost? Who isn't? And where? In the woods. In a labyrinth. Without Ariadne threads of discourse which one must learn to use—everyone has his head full of them—one cannot find his way. *It is the art of removal, of riddance.* And what does one get rid of? Of temptations. What temptations? Not bottles, except on occasion and then it is not the bottle which is the temptation, which any fly would like to be in a position to tell you. "I have been trying in all this to remove the temptation to think that there must be . . ." (p. 41). *It is the art of discussion.* For what purpose? To show differences. One might be inclined to say that whereas Socrates practiced and taught the art of discussion for the sake of seeking what is common, this author practiced and taught the art of discussion in order to restore the balance, to correct distortion, stressing differences. And what is the art of discussion? It is the art of presenting meaning. *It is the art of exposure.* Exposing what? Hidden analogies. As there are hidden motives, not hidden by but hidden even from those whose motives they are, and these are helpful in explaining what people do when they are themselves persuaded, so too there are hidden analogies which are not noticed by those on whose behalf they are appealed to to explain what they say. *It is the art of helpful reminders.* For what purpose? When your words seem to carry you along so that you seem to have lost the reins and you lose your head to the words, then, if you pause, reminding yourself of how words are harnessed together to do the speaker's work, then you regain control. Runaway language.

It is the art of working puzzles. Cross-word puzzles? No, not cross-word puzzles but word puzzles. The author's analogy is with jig-saw puzzles. "It's no use trying to apply force in fitting pieces together. All we should do is to look at them carefully and arrange them" (p. 46). Presumably there are sentences or rather arrangements of words which puzzle us because the words are jumbled, though not in such a way as immediately to strike us as jumbled. So we may ask: Are they jumbled? And then we rearrange them and get them in order. *It is the art of scrutinizing the grammar of a word.* Naturally this is to serve a purpose. If we recall that it is in terms of the grammar of a word, some particularly relevant part of the context of a word, that we present to ourselves that aspect of the meaning of a word we need in order to bring to light some deviation from the grammar of the word, into which we may have drifted or fallen, we can understand the service of such scrutiny. *It is the art of freeing us from illusions.* Illusions? Yes, illusions of a special sort, illusions of sense where there is no sense. And how are we freed from illusions? By looking more closely. So in this case we look more closely at the sentence or sentences with respect to which we are deceived. And how, then, do we look more closely? Obviously it is not a matter of looking more closely at the words on the page. What we are to see looking more closely is that the words as they are put together here, perhaps not only in this sentence but in these surroundings, cease to have the meaning which they have in the surroundings in which they have meaning. And no other meaning has been given. *It is the art of the detective.* The author also describes what he does as "investigations." "In fact one may say that what in these investigations we were concerned with . . ." (p. 70). A detective is one who surveys the scene, notices details, picks up scraps, fragments, piecing them together in order to get some idea, a picture of what happened. With every new clue he gets a new picture or a completer picture. He abandons clues, and seizes upon new ones. He is frequently like a man groping in the dark. And the art of the investigator taught in these dictations also surveys the language scene, looking for clues, hitting on this, guessing here, in order to explain the deviation, the unwitting deviation, from sense. "So this is what misled me." But what he must hit upon is the explanation which will satisfy the thinker who was himself misled. Until he has done this he is not freed. This analogy is intended to stress that there is no straight line of investigation. Cases here may be as baffling and complicated as cases which the detective investigates. It would, however, be misleading to say that the investigator also tries to get a picture of what happened. He has nothing to investigate but the language. And that is not a happening. *It is the art of clarification, of relief from the toils of confusion.* What confusion? Grammatical confusion. There is strife among these words that will not lie down together and that keep up this turmoil in our heads. And there will be no rest until we put each word into its own bed.

That fly that was let out of the fly-bottle understands how he got in there, since the condition of his being let out is that he should understand that. And now he can fly in and out as he likes. It is no longer a fly-bottle for him. He can now buzz in and out enjoying the structure of the bottle. A fun-bottle, then? Yes, until he finds himself in another bottle with a different opening. Eternal vigilance is the price of buzzing freely.

The variety among these descriptions may suggest to us something of the complexity of the art which the author set out to teach. It is, however, unlikely that, apart from the practice of it in the examination of particular cases which constitutes the main body of The Blue Book, these descriptions will be helpful. For it is the author himself who introduced these descriptions in order to help these students to get the point of what he was doing. So the presence of these descriptions for that purpose also suggests how difficult he must have found trying to teach this to others. Now, however, I should like to give an account, perhaps misleadingly simple, of what the author does in this book. On page 16 is the sentence: "I shall propose to you to look closely at particular cases . . . ," and what I want to give an account of is what the author does looking closely. If what I now go on to say is simple, this should not lead one to suppose that to do what he does is either simple or easy.

One may, as I think, distinguish in the art I have been describing three phases or moments. I hesitate to say that there are three things which he does. And I do not mean to say that in looking closely at any particular case all three phases can be distinguished or that there is this systematic arrangement, one, two, three, which he follows. There is not. I mean rather that whenever he is looking closely at some particular case he will be engaged in one of these three phases or moments. And I have intentionally used the words "phases" or "moments" to avoid the mistake of supposing that some exact line could be drawn between them. The three phases I have in mind are these: First, the author seeks to quicken the sense of the queer. Second, the author is concerned to present the meaning of those expressions which are involved in the particular case, and especially those which are relevant to exhibiting not the queerness but the sources, the roots of it. Third, the author seeks to uncover the "misleading analogy." These phases or objectives are not pursued in any such order, though they may be, but it may well be that one's sense of the queer is quickened by the presentation of the meaning and even more by the uncovering of "the misleading analogy."

I want to explain each of these.

It is quite obvious that, except for a few extraordinary cases, philosophical questions do not strike us as queer. Perhaps to begin with a question like: Do I exist? or Do I alone exist? or Do forests murmur? may strike a young ear or an untutored ear as queer, but such questions as What is knowledge? or Does God exist? or How is science possible? are not likely to strike either a young ear or an old ear as queer. Accordingly if the beginning of intelligence lies here it is obvious that a great deal of work must be done with spoiled ears. They do not hear the queer. The queerness of the questions must be made to ring. And so the author must make it ring. There are presumably a number of ways. Sometimes it is sufficient or at least helpful to draw attention to the queerness. "Now, listen to the question: What is the meaning of a word? Can't you hear that's queer?" And then if someone strains to hear he will hear it queer like a shadow passing over the question. There are other ways. If there are questions which have already struck one as queer and these questions are heard now side by side with the other question, the queerness of these questions may, as it were, be communicated to the other question, like vibrations. And if there are no familiar questions which one may employ to bring out the queerness of the first one, then one may invest some questions in which the queerness is as loud as a bang. "What is the color of the number three?" Does unconscious tooth-ache hurt in the unconscious more, or less, than conscious tooth-ache hurts in consciousness? Of course, one must exercise a nice judgment here, inventing only what is adapted to the necessities of the case. It may be a mistake to invent a question whose queerness is loud as a bang. One may need queerness that whispers, barely audible, sufficient to provide the right nuance. There are other ways, such as giving an answer intended to echo the form of queerness in the question. "Thinking is a process which goes on invisibly in your feet while you are busy making words at the other end of the line." "Why in the feet?" "Well, why not?" But one may also accentuate the queerness by the contrast with the unqueer. You ask: What is the meaning of a word? and do not know what to say. But when I ask you: What is the meaning of the word "ogre"? you tell me. So you do know what the meaning of a word is, namely, the word "ogre." So what is it you do not know? It should be obvious that what is done in such cases is to play with the similarities and differences among whatever forms of sense and sentences may serve the purpose.

And now I want to go on to the second phase, the presentation of meaning. If we regard the queerness discussed in the preceding paragraph as an impression of a sometimes scarcely perceptible deviation from sense, then we may appreciate the author's interest in presenting the sense. For in that case what is involved is a contrast between what is regarded as a deviation and some sense or other also of course heard or seen. Something is not quite right. Perhaps the word "difference" is a better word than "contrast." What accordingly we have is either sense in the guise of nonsense or nonsense in the guise of sense. It sounds like sense and it sounds like nonsense. It cannot in any particular case be both. If a question sounds queer then it will not be surprising if it turns out to be nonsensical. And if it turns out to make sense then some special explanation will be needed to show this sense. There may be some analogy one has missed. "The child is father of the man," "Go and catch a falling star." In any case if this is how the queerness is to be regarded, then in order to understand it, it will be necessary to exhibit the sense from which the sentence or sentences are a deviation. The principle involved is simple. Some words together in a certain order, taken together with other words, etc., make sense and the same words taken together with certain other words in a certain order do not make sense. So what we need is to remind ourselves of the sense of the words which make up the queer sentence in order to see precisely what the deviation, what the difference is.

And how now does one present the sense?

Presenting the sense must not be confused with giving the meaning. If someone does not know the meaning of a word then you explain the meaning to him. But presenting the sense is not like that. If you know the meaning then you can present the sense. And this consists in reminding oneself of what one says, the lay of the lingo in the surroundings of this or that word, what words, sentences, go together with the word or expression about which one is concerned. I consider it absolutely magnificent that a man should have conceived of the idea that you can present to yourself the meaning of a word. And yet, it turns out to be so simple. That one is able to do this provides the perspective which makes possible the comparisons and contrasts by means of which similarities and differences are discernible. For what holds of the delineation of sense holds also of the delineation of nonsense. The point in presenting the meaning is not to present the meaning complete—even in a dead language meaning is not complete—but to present so much of the meaning as is required for whatever the purpose may be.

The third phase is that of uncovering the "misleading analogy." If it is allowed that the queerness which the author is concerned with is that of nonsense in the guise of sense, then we may conceive of the task involved as two-fold, namely, to

exhibit the nonsense, the deviation from sense, and to explain
the illusion of sense. How is it that one should have come to ask
this or to say this in the first place, and that one should hold on
so tenaciously? There are a number of analogies we may notice
in the book: "We try to find a substance for a substantive" (p. 1);
"The contradiction which here seems to arise could be called a
conflict between two different usages of a word, in this case, the
word 'measure'" (p. 26); "the existence of the words 'thinking'
and 'thought' alongside of the words denoting (bodily) activities,
such as writing, speaking, etc., makes us look for an activity,
different from these but analogous to them, corresponding to the
word 'thinking,'" (p. 7) etc. Uncovering the misleading analogy
helps one to explain the hold of these questions upon us. Hector
was dragged around the city of Troy by a horse. But we are
dragged around by hidden analogies and most of all if we think.
This is how it comes about that sometimes the best advice is:
"Don't think. Look." And it may be hard not to think.

The author has the following explanation of the misleading
analogy: "The cases in which particularly we wish to say that
someone is misled by a form of expression are those in which we
would say: 'he wouldn't talk as he does if he were aware of this
difference in the grammar of such-and-such words, or if he
were aware of this other possibility of expression'" (p. 28). It
may be helpful to add that if today he wouldn't then tomorrow
when he is aware, he won't. The point is that the object is not a
science of misleading expressions from which one can now
figure out what is misleading some stranger. The object is to
assist some individual, always an individual, to help him discover
what misleads and has misled him. And what misled him is to be
seen only when he is no longer misled. When he says: "Now, I
see" and breathes a sigh of relief, even though it may be a bit
sheepishly, that is the moment to which the art is directed.

Here we may take notice of the analogy with psychoanalysis.
We might say in connection with psychoanalysis: "He wouldn't
do as he does if he were aware of what it is in his past that he
has forgotten that now drives him to do this." And the art in

this case is devoted to refreshing his memory and to bringing him round to where he says, "That is it," and now he doesn't do it anymore. This is cure. In the case of both those who talk as they do and those who do as they do, the explanation is not to be sought in asking them. They find out only as by cure they also cease to talk so and to do so. Beyond this the analogy does not go. In the case of psychoanalysis it is the past, the materials of memory, both lost but retrievable, and not lost, which one tries to bring back, to discover the moving cause, something hidden. But in the case of "he wouldn't talk as he does" one does not investigate anyone's past. One investigates the language and a particular area of that, and that is much more like investigating a familiar part of one's environment, which is also the environment of all of us. There is nothing sticky about this investigation, no private dirty linen shook and washed in private or in public.

There is one further point. The misleading analogy is hidden. It is present in the language and not hidden there. It is, however, hidden from the person who is misled by it. Hence it isn't as though he attended carefully to the analogy and went on from there with his eyes open. In that case he could tell us that he was following an analogy. But he knows nothing about it. All the same he keeps bumping his head against it. Relieving him consists in getting him to recognize the analogy that has misled him. And what are the clues? His question, and what he goes on to say in explaining and answering the question will bear the marks of the analogy. There are forms of bewilderment too.

I have now given an account of the art which, as I conceive it, the author of this book teaches in three phases. It is carried on by discussion, either in writing or orally. There is commonly a helper and helped, though obviously several people may help one another. The queer is seen to be queerer and queerer. Ideas mingled throw up a mist and when by way of discussion, catalytic agent, the ideas fall apart, the mist is cleared away.

I have already referred to the complexity and the difficulty of teaching this art. And how does one go about teaching an art?

No doubt, by practicing it and in such a way that the learner can observe what the teacher is doing. In teaching someone to use his hands, in carpentry for instance, the learner observes how the teacher holds the tools and what he does with each. He learns by doing what the teacher does. The teacher also observes what the learner does and now and then corrects him. Of course the learner understands that he is building a house and why he does what he does. He did not have to be told what carpentry is. Didn't he come to the carpenter and say, "Teach me to be a carpenter"? How different it is with these students! They could have had no idea what the art was that he would teach them and perhaps had no idea that he was to teach them an art. They had more likely come to him expecting that he would answer their questions. Perhaps they asked him: What is the meaning of a word? or What is thinking? So he, unlike the carpenter, had not simply to teach them an art with which they were well-acquainted, but he had to introduce them to an art of which they had not heard and for which they could have felt no need. Hence, even if he had stood before them and said: "Now, pay close attention to what I am doing" and had then gone on to practice his art as he does in those early pages, is it likely that they would have understood? He is, remember, teaching an art which is new. He is the author, the inventor, the first teacher. But why should an art which is new be so difficult to teach? It isn't like working with new materials, plastics, for instance, supposing that were difficult. Why cannot the teacher tell them plainly what he is going to teach and then teach it? The art is a language-art and there is nothing new about that. Nevertheless, anyone who reads this book can see with what diligence and patience the author tried to get these students to understand him. This explains his varied attempts by analogy to tell them. And it explains, too, his attempts to show them and to help them over the difficulties which he realized hindered them.

I want now to emphasize the difficulties, taking notice of them in each of the phases.

There are in the first phase two sorts of difficulties, those

involved in following what the author does and those involved in
doing what he does. Consider the case in which the author
considers: "How can one think what is not the case?" He
introduces for comparison the sentence: "How can we hang a
thief who doesn't exist?" He does this to startle one into an
appreciation of the queerness of the first question and to show,
too, what sort of queerness is involved. There is a part of this
which seems not difficult. The sentence which is introduced
certainly is a queer one. Another one which is queer is: "Can
a machine have tooth-ache?" And most readers are likely to be
amused by such antics. But this, of course, is not the point. It
isn't the queerness of those sentences which interests the author.
The question is as to whether the queerness of these sentences
helps to bring to light the queerness of the sentences considered.
For those sentences are regarded as grammatically confused,
and the sentences with which they are compared are intended to
stress this confusion. The question: Can a machine have tooth-
ache? is grammatically confused in the same way that: Can a
machine think? is. Any yet one might very well retort: Perhaps a
machine cannot have tooth-ache, but it seems a machine can
think. And this may be alarming. Who wants to be mechanical
and to have tooth-ache? So, too, the question: How can we hang
a thief who doesn't exist? (It seems we can hang a thief who
doesn't exist—in effigy, and that suits people, too, who figure
out a way of thinking what is not the case. They think the
effigies.) is intended to show the queerness of: How can we think
what is not the case? But in order to get the full impact of this,
one must have some nice sense of the grammar and of the
confusions involved, which one may come by naturally, being
meaning-keen, or may come by with special instruction. It is
only with special instruction that one can understand what is
being done. And that will involve those difficulties one meets in
the other two phases.

As for the difficulties involved in doing what the author does,
inventing such devices, I scarcely know what to say. If you are
something of a poet you may certainly learn from the poets,

though even this does not mean that writing poems will be easy. And if you are nothing of a poet then though you may love poems, you cannot do as the poets do with or without difficulties.

Consider difficulties involved in understanding what Wittgenstein does under the second phase. It would seem that anyone can do in this case what is required. For all that one needs to do is to remember what people as a matter of fact do say. You speak English. You understand English. You know what goes with what, the continuities of sense. Of course. But what at the outset is difficult is to take this, these words, these sentences, as the presentation of sense. For one has, as it were, for years been looking through the words, into the darkness, the *hinein*, where no man can follow, for the meaning. That is what stirs in the question: What is the meaning of a word? Hence, even though someone now emphasizes: "But this is the meaning," this may not help. It may all pass before one like a blur. Let us suppose, however, that one has finally overcome this difficulty, not that it does not return, but one does have one's moments. All this is done for a purpose. The presentation of meaning, of such aspects as are required, serves in at least two ways, to accentuate the queerness and to provide the area within which the misleading analogy is to be identified. None of this, remember, is a matter of rules, or of self-evidence, so beloved of many, foundations of security. No one proves that this question is queer, or that in the sentence "But you can look for a thief who isn't there" or "But you can be afraid of a little man who isn't there" meaning is presented, or that if it is presented it does serve in the ways described. Let us suppose, however, that when the author has now done this in some cases, that one also understands this, can follow what he has done. Does this, however, involve that one can now on one's own do likewise? Obviously not. What do we lack?

And now the third phase, identifying "the misleading analogy." If the first ideas involved here are strange, new, and difficult, the third is too, and is unintelligible apart from them. For the misleading analogy explains the hold which the queer has upon us. And I think that this is fearfully difficult and from another point of view fantastically simple. Suppose I say that the meaning of a word is a sort of something, vegetable, animal, or mineral, no, but not a gas either, nor a liquid; but why should it not be something paraphysical, for instance, if you call a word physical, mineral or a gas, in which case you might say that it is either para-mineral or para-gas? This sentence makes it much too clear that I am thinking of meaning as a thing for even me to have the illusion of thinking it. Let us disregard that. Let us suppose further that someone is startled by this. He exclaims: "Why, he is thinking of meaning as a thing!" and now comes the question: "But what leads him to do this?" It is no answer to say: "Everybody does." For here is at least one person who for the moment does not. And now comes the answer: Naturally enough because the expression "the meaning of a word," is like the expression "the king of a country," and the king of a country is a thing, animal, has weight, lives on air, meat, vegetables, noise, etc., so the question arises: what sort of thing is the meaning of a word, no animal, imponderable, neither living nor dead? Now I do not know whether it is difficult to tumble to so simple an explanation of what seems, when one is involved in it, so fearfully intricate. It almost seems as though something like a change of heart is required for this. It is well nigh miraculous, like opening ten-ton doors with a feather. For isn't it ridiculously simple? You think of meaning in a certain way and you find yourself all fenced in ("Don't fence me in"), and how now did you come to do this? There was an expression which looked like another expression, and misled by this you went on as though their meanings, too, were analogous. How does one tumble in a case like this? Perhaps one can set oneself in readiness. "Relax. Don't resist." And is that so easy? Haven't we inherited the tensions of all those generations before us? Original (the inherited) knots and besides original knots, original knots. One's nature is knots. In any case it is that simple. If only there were some complicated explanation, ladders and ladders of explanation, an architectural mystery-piece of calculation, that would suit our natural bent.

Learning to do what the author teaches may in some respects

be compared to learning to walk. There are certain to be bumps and falls. One must want to learn. But there are no special resources required. Nearly everyone can and does learn to walk. So, too, in this case. One must try when one can't do. One must risk stupidities and clumsiness and misunderstandings. One must be patient and diligent. Above all one must want to do the doing of which is here taught. And no special resources are required. What is required is an acquaintance with the language, an eye and an ear for sense. This is a requirement and may be compared to the musical ear in the case of music. This man can scarcely make out differences in tone. He has never heard a melody. So he can't study music. And there does seem to be something comparable in the case of reading philosophy. To some readers everything makes sense. What the author of this book does may be described in this way. The students lend him their eyes and ears for sense and he tries to sharpen them, tries to make them keen. "I will show you how to see and hear sense." And are no special talents required? It seems that there are.

The one obvious and pervading difficulty in reading this book and one against which one must struggle continually as soon as he understands the danger is the temptation to misunderstanding the very book which is designed to help us to remove temptation to misunderstandings in other circumstances. I try to persuade you not to steal at the grocery store and in doing so tempt you to steal from me. The hankering for orderliness, for system, for summaries is a general aspect of this. (What is the man doing? He's putting three books together on the shelf [p. 44].) But it may also be remarked in the way in which certain sentences are widely misunderstood. The temptation here arises from one's coming upon a sentence the like of which one had perhaps met in some other context and one goes on to read it now in terms of that context, utterly oblivious of the immediate context in which it is found. There are two such sentences which I should like to point out.

The first of these sentences is the one at the bottom of page 4: "But if we had to name anything which is the life of the sign, we should have to say that it was its use." This sentence apart from the "if we had to" and "we should have to," looks like a definition. "The life of the sign" is, of course, the meaning. So, how convenient this is that the author, in spite of himself, should have yielded and given us what we so much want: The meaning of a word is its use. No sentence has more powerfully formed the jargon of contemporary discussion in philosophy. Nearly everyone these days speaks and writes in this new fashion. And yet nothing has been changed. If before we were puzzled with: What is the meaning of a word? now we are puzzled with: What is the use of a word? (I think I paced up and down in this cage for years.) Having made a puzzle out of this we ask such further questions as how the author came upon such a definition. What English teacher would ever allow the interchange of the words "meaning" and "use"? As a definition the sentence is indefensible and if it is defensible, what good comes of it? Locke speaks of "use" but to what advantage? Some people have even been misled into identifying the statement with some old or new Pragmatism.

But what then?

The author on page 67 writes: "Think of words as instruments characterized by their use, and then think of the use of a hammer, the use of a chisel, the use of a square, of glue-pot, and of the glue." One can see from this how the sentence on page 4 is to be understood. It is intended not as a definition but as an analogy or if as a definition, then as a definition of a special sort. In the latter case it comes to something like this: If you will say "use" and write "use" instead of "meaning" in writing and speaking of words, and can manage to think accordingly, that will help. Help what? It will help you to rid yourself of the temptation to think of the meaning as something in the dark which you cannot see very well. The idea is that if your thinking is dominated in this case by one misleading analogy then you may be led right by another leading analogy. If, of course, that second analogy also misleads one, not much may be gained. But as long as one is well aware of the analogy and what it is for, it should do its work. And it should now help one to see what the role of a word is in the various circumstances of our lives in which we speak and write that word together, of course, with other words. And if we allow that we understand the word, are acquainted with the meaning, then this is where it is to be found, since this is all we know. So we may understand that sentence as one which is intended to help us to a change in perspective. Once that change has come about, the sentence, like the ladder, is of no further use.

The other sentence is the sentence on page 28, "But ordinary language is all right." The same temptation which gave rise to misunderstanding in the former case gives rise to misunderstanding in this case. The immediate context of the sentence is disregarded and the sentence is understood as stating some philosophical theory, perhaps naive. And in this way it, too, has affected current jargon. There are ordinary language philosophers. People now go on with all sorts of difficult questions. They want to know just what ordinary language is and whether it really is a language and how one can decide that without first finding out what a language is. And then, of course, there's still the question as to whether it is all right. It seems that no one with any conscience could speak so carelessly. But what now is the situation? It comes to this. Some philosophers, particularly those who love mathematics more than poetry, are struck, when they read the newspaper or listen to the conversation at dinner, with the disorder of the language. The conversation at dinner is certainly not Euclidean. Perhaps one can imagine some lovers of poetry also who when reading the newspaper or listening to conversation at dinner remark that no verse should be that free. So the mathematicians, as a first step, propose some rules. Conversational deduction is to come later. And perhaps the lovers of poetry introduce measures and some rudiments of drill, marching, leaping, sprinting, waltzing, to make the news less pedestrian. In protection against this someone comes along and reads an excerpt from the newspaper. He asks: "What is the matter with that? So the man did catch the monkey in the subway." Again he asks: "And what is the matter with trying to get the little boy who says wove for love and wanded for landed to say love for wove and landed for wanded? He now says that the airpwane wanded. A little free verse here does no harm. And more doesn't either." The mathematicians frown. The poets frown too. Now, this is approximately what the author's sentence comes to. "Ordinary language is all right." The grocer understands the boy when the boy gives him the money and asks for five apples. The grocer's bawd understands what the grocer says when he says and pats her cheek. And the grocer's bawd's sister understands what the grocer's bawd says when she says: "And what are the neighbors saying now?" And the neighbors understand one another. And so on. Ordinary language is all right? Of course, we understand one another. The question is: What are all those rules for? And the shackles on the verse? There is nothing mysterious about the author's sentence when seen against the background of prejudice which gives rise to it.

When Protagoras was consulted about what would happen to the young Hippocrates if he associated with Protagoras, Protagoras answered: "Young man, if you associate with me, on the very first day you will return home a better man than you came, and better on the second day than on the first and better every day than you were on the day before." And if now we were to ask concerning some young Hippocrates from Harvard or Yale what would happen to him if he reads this book, we should certainly not with the courage of Protagoras' convictions say anything like what Protagoras said. Let us try a few answers. "Young man, if you read this book as you read most books nothing whatsoever will happen to you and it won't take long. On the very first day you will return home a no-better man than you came, on the second day the same, and so on." Or: "Young man, if you read this book diligently, digging as you are used to digging in the books you read, coming up with a shining truth here and a nice bristling idea there, the chances are that you will have got it all wrong. You will go home full of indigestibles, and oh, the pity of it! a worse man than you came, not much worse, but let us say, four or five misunderstandings worse." Or: "Young man, if you read this book with your mind wide open, and take time to stew in it or to let it stew in you; if with a little bit of luck, it should cling to you like a bramble and it should hurt and sting and all the while the agitations keep you alert, then inkling by inkling, glimpse by glimpse, chink by chink, on the very first day ten years later, you will return home a different man than you came."

And what now are intelligible reactions to this book? Since this book as here represented, at least, aims to teach its readers how to do a certain thing, one obvious reaction is this: "We don't want it done." I say that this is intelligible so long as no reasons are given. As a blind reaction it's fine. But how is one to give reasons? Is one to say: "Yes, yes, we admit the grammatical confusion and the misleading analogy, but what we ask and say makes sense anyhow"? Has anyone given such a reason? The other reaction is this: "We want it done. But we want it done better." It seems that it could be done better. This comment no doubt reflects the impression of incoherence referred to earlier. It may also reflect a failure to recognize the almost overwhelming obstacles involved. For one has not simply to present the particular cases, one has also to help the reader to understand the presentation and to clear away the obstacles to understanding. These different tasks, which are all necessary, make it impossible to proceed in a straight line. There is, however, something even more telling. The presentation of a case is nothing neatly defined. The grammars of different words are interwoven and the presentation of the particular case is bound to reflect the incoherence of the language. Perhaps one could express it in this way: The coherence of the language, the criss-crossing of the grammar of the words we are interested in, is quite different from the coherence of words in a certain language game, in a story, or in an essay. (A good illustration of this is the discussion beginning on page 6 to the bottom of page 15.) This is not to say that the coherence of this book is loose but rather that the orderliness of this book is determined by the variety of the tasks and by the particular sort of complexity of the materials. One might also take note here of what either are or seem to be obvious mistakes in the presentation of a case, and it might be a good test of one's reading of the book that he should be able to discover those mistakes. I do not think, however, that the presence of these mistakes affects the pedagogical efficacy of the book. It may actually enhance it.

Towards the end of Moore's notes on Wittgenstein's Lectures in 1930–33, is the following paragraph:

> He went on to say that, though philosophy had now been "reduced to a matter of skill," yet this skill, like other skills, is very difficult to acquire. One difficulty was that it required a "sort of thinking" to which we are not accustomed and to which we have not been trained—a sort of thing very different from what is required in the sciences. And he said that the required skill could not be acquired merely by hearing lectures: discussion was essential. As regards his own work, he said it did not matter whether his results were true or not: what mattered was that "a method had been found." [1]

Though I came upon this passage only after I had written this piece, what I have written might be described as an elaboration of the contents of this paragraph.

[1] G. E. Moore, "Wittgenstein's Lectures in 1930–33," *Mind*, Vol. LXIV, No. 253 (January, 1955), p. 26.

THE TERMS OF ORDINARY
LANGUAGE ARE...*

"···when the skeptic Zeno pursued the study of
skepticism by endeavoring to keep himself un-
affected by whatever happened, so that when once
he had gone out of his way to avoid a mad dog,
he shamefacedly admitted that even a skeptical
philosopher is also sometimes a man···"

Kierkegaard

THE SENTENCE I PROPOSE TO DISCUSS in these notes is the
sentence "The terms of ordinary language are notoriously
ambiguous and vague." I consider this sentence crucial.

Having reminded you of this sentence, I want first of all to
ask concerning the paper Maxwell has read to you: Is it written
in ordinary English? There is good reason to say that it is. On
the first page you will find the words "we"—Could any word
be more ambiguous and vague?—by their standards, I mean—
"we," "drunkards," "reprobates," "city charters" (perhaps
that should have been "city slickers"). If it is written in ordinary
English, the terms in it are ambiguous and vague, and no one
could be expected to understand it. But if it is not written in
ordinary English, then, the prospect is no better. For the
definitions, rules, and postulates are not provided, and what can
we do without those? This question may suggest to you how
crucial that sentence about the terms of ordinary language is. I

* This paper was read some time ago at a meeting of the Western Division of
The American Philosophical Association as a part of a symposium. This paper was
in response to a longer paper by Messrs Feigl and Maxwell, a paper subsequently
published in the Journal of Philosophy.

will go on now to treat that sentence as one in ordinary English and so will fail to understand it just as they said I would. I will proceed then to try to figure out how to understand the unintelligibility of it. There is one word in it, namely, the word "notoriously" which gives me no trouble. I understand it in this way: Feigl told Maxwell and Maxwell told June and June told Feigl, and that's how it got all around. The problem may be stated in this way. Who told Feigl? or How did Feigl find out?

Before I go on I am going to introduce certain examples of ordinary language to make sure we understand what terms Feigl and Maxwell are writing about.

I will begin with something extremely simple. First, there is Mrs. Protheroe who calls her chickens. She calls "chick, chick, chick," and the chickens run and fly to her. "They all ran after the farmer's wife." Then she feeds them. Second, there is Maxwell who reads the story of the Three Little Pigs to his three little daughters, all twins, Elsie and Tillie and Lucey. They sit crowded close to him and listen as he reads and when Maxwell comes to the part "and he huffed and he puffed," they all join in, huffing and puffing, even Maxwell, who, as you will come to see, seems at the same time, not to understand a word he reads. Then, they all laugh. They do not like the wolf but they love the three little pigs. Third is that great classic of ordinary language, the Sears-Roebuck catalogue. People know what they want, they have money to buy what they want. They study the catalogue, they make out the order, send it off with check enclosed, and someone, Mr. or Mrs. Sears, reads the order, puts the underwear in a box and sends it to the Institute. It gets cold in Minneapolis.

So you see what a task of reform Feigl and Maxwell have taken upon themselves. But it really is their own idea. No one asked them to do it, not Mrs. Protheroe, not the three Maxwell sisters, and not Sears-Roebuck. Think of it: All the terms in the Sears-Roebuck catalogue ambiguous and vague! But whose language is it, anyhow, that they should take it upon themselves to change it?

In order to help you to get some perspective of what Feigl and Maxwell seem to be saying, imagine a linguistic cataclysm, something like what happened at the tower of Babel. Perhaps you remember the scripture "Come, let us go down, and then confuse their language that they may not understand one another's speech." Presumably, in this case God took away their definitions, their rules, and their postulates, and the consequence was that the terms of their ordinary—or was it, then, extra-ordinary?—language, were on that day in May suddenly ambiguous and vague. I want, however, a limited cataclysm. It happens in the night and the next day the terms in Mrs. Protheroe's chicken-call, in the story of the Three Little Pigs, and the Sears-Roebuck catalogue are ambiguous and vague. We can leave the rest of the language as it is. The cataclysm is selective. That morning Mrs. Protheroe as usual goes out to call her chickens. She calls "chick, chick, chick," and what happens? Some chickens run, some this way, some that way, some sit down, resting, others sit down on their tails, turning and doing tricks, some begin scratching, and some go round-and-round, and some go back and forth, and some run to Mrs. Protheroe and begin to sing. Mrs. Protheroe laughs. She calls the neighbors. She says: "Come, my chickens have lost their minds." And so it is. And now, let us see how it is with Maxwell who reads the story of the Three Little Pigs to his three little girls. In the midst of the reading little Elsie breaks in with: "Oh, daddy, we don't understand that story anymore. All the words, except the in-between words are ambiguous and vague, so vague we don't even know what the ambiguity is, and so clearly ambiguous we can't make out how they are vague. Without those words we can't even understand the in-between words. All the children in school were talking about it today. They all remember there was a story but they don't understand it any-more. They say it sounds just like so much mutter. It's notorious now. Could you fix it, daddy? Daddy, what's 'huff and puff?'" And Maxwell said that the words sounded familiar to him but that he had never understood them anyhow. He was sorry, however, that they too did not understand them now, and he read in that book no more that day.

As for what the cataclysm did to the catalogue, what a time they had of it at Sears'. All the terms ambiguous and vague! They couldn't fill an order right. A man seemed to want a rake and they gave him socks. It was all guess-work. People were returning articles they never wanted for others they never wanted. No one could say what he wanted and no one else could make out what it was he wasn't saying. It was exasperating. People made hands do what words wouldn't, and got their rakes. But in this case even money couldn't talk. Dollars made no sense. At one o'clock Sears-Roebuck shut up shop, and as at the Tower of Babel, Montgomery-Ward took over the business.

Now is this how it looks to Feigl and Maxwell? Are they in one of their prophetic moods still writing ordinary language and writing about the end of the world, a non-selective cataclysm?

I want to make sure of this and so I ask you: If you were one of these empirically-minded eye-openers, opening the eyes of all of us, and had some of the bug of science in your mentality and wanted to find out whether the terms of ordinary language are ambiguous, what would you do? Would you look into the horse's mouth? I am now going to propose an expedient. Get the dictionary and see for yourself whether among the words entered on some page there are any words for which the explainer gives but one explanation. Let me tell you what I found on page 1. The first word "a" is followed by twelve different explanations. It is a first-rate abomination. I expect that when Feigl and Maxwell get around to it they will lop off eleven of those. Then follow the words "A-1," "a'-a," "aam," "aardvark," "aardwolf," each with but one meaning. Then follow "Aaron" with three, "Aaronic" with one, "Aaronical" with two, "Aaron's-beard" with one, "Aaron's rod" with three, but "Ab," the next, with one—"the fifth month of the Jewish ecclesiastical year"—, then, "ab" with one, "aba" with two, "abaca" with one, "abacist" with one. So much for page 1. And how now did

Feigl find out that the terms of ordinary language are ambiguous and vague? It seems that he turned his head the other way.

It must be clear by now that Feigl and Maxwell are not writing ordinary English. On the assumption that they were, I asked the question: How did Feigl find this out? Now, however, I want to ask a different question: What has led Feigl and Maxwell to say this?

I am going to risk the following true explanation.

You will remember that Don Quixote after reading too many romances, "a one-sided diet," began to see everything through the spectacles of what he had read. He saw windmills as giants, serving maids as princesses, barber's basins as golden helmets, inns as castles. You could scarcely say that he saw the windmills, the serving maids, etc. And now this is not at all how it is with Feigl and Maxwell, at least not very much, though somewhat, and perhaps more than you would expect. For whereas Don Quixote read romances and consequently saw windmills as giants, and whereas Feigl and Maxwell certainly do read science, yet it cannot be said that they see windmills as giants or anything like that; nevertheless, it must be said that they read science and do see ordinary language through the spectacles of the language of certain science. And you can scarcely say that they ever see ordinary language, Mrs. Protheroe's call, the story, or the catalogue.

In order to explain this let me remind you of what reading geometry is like. If in reading Euclid you come upon a term you do not understand, on page 70, then you can turn back to page 3 and find there the definitions, rules, and postulates, strictly determining what you can do with that word in the system. And if some word turned up for which no such provision had been made, the word "chick," for instance, that word would have to be scratched or provision made. It would be deleted or incorporated into the system. Now notice what seems to have happened. After years of reading geometry and after only some reading of the story of the Three Little Pigs, Maxwell one day comes to page 70 of the story of the Three Little Pigs, and upon the word "pig"—it suddenly strikes him—and he automatically turns to page 3 to find the definitions, rules, and postulates. He is amazed. What, no rules! You can't have a language without rules! He brings his troubles to Feigl and together they worry about the rules. They make rules, rules for all the terms. When they have finished, the philosophical purpose is realized. And now for whom are these rules made? Well, naturally, for Mrs. Protheroe, for Maxwell, the reader;—now he will be able to read with expression—; and for Sears-Roebuck, the seller. Do they pay attention? Not a bit. If Feigl tells Mrs. Protheroe she can't call the chickens without rules, or if she can't state the rules or if Feigl can't, she says that the chickens haven't been told and so they come anyhow. And what about Maxwell's three little girls and all the customers? They, too, oh so ignorantly understand. But this is what comes of regarding ordinary language as wanton geometry. Geometry, the hussy sent to the Feigl home of correction. And now you can see clearly what the philosophical purpose is. The purpose is to regard ordinary language as geometry. In that way, according to Feigl and Maxwell, you generate philosophical problems. This explanation might also serve to show someone how to avoid something. And what about all those rules? They are obviously an embarrassment of riches. Riches and no need.

Is it more fantastic on the part of Don Quixote to mistake windmills for giants than for Feigl and Maxwell to mistake ordinary language for geometry? Suppose that someone proposed to make the story of the Three Little Pigs sound like the proof of the Pythagorean theorem, with all the preliminary clutter concerning the hypotenuse of the third little pig and the tangent drawn to the curl in the wolf's tail. Mixed up? Only a detail made up out of the general mix-up. If you look at all terms in ordinary language as designed for the purpose of proof, that's what you get.

Imagine the following. Someone, Bergson, perhaps, mistakes geometry for ordinary language. He is shocked. What! No tenses? A language without provision for so pervasive a feature of our world? It's preposterous. And what about the psychological verbs? We need triangles that think and hope and call the chickens and cry. Geometry as at present constituted is dumb. And think of it, no personal pronouns! We can't say "Feigl" in geometry. This man is about to get rid of geometry. And then? Then along come the reformers, Feigl and Maxwell, from the other side. They write an essay on the subject: Why geometry needs reformation for philosophical purposes. And the complaint? That the terms of geometry are tied down to rules. They suffer the embarrassments of poverty. They love freedom. They propose to loosen things up a bit. There is to be a rich assortment of ambiguous terms, some in twelve variations. There are to be a few vague words, to get in lines "almost" straight. They are going to wreck geometry, but are determined to make it adaptable to telling the story of the Three Little Pigs and to anything else anyone would ever like to say about pigs, things said already, and things not yet said. Needless to say, they also do not succeed. All the changes they ever make are marks in their note-books. Euclid continues to mock their efforts. Still what they try to do, loosening up things a bit in geometry, corresponds nicely to what the other Feigl and Maxwell proposed to do, namely, tightening up things a bit in ordinary English. Will the Queen heed their wise counsels? Will the President?

And now to return to my original question: Is it written in ordinary language? I have answered: No. Is it then written in some other language? I will leave that question open. Any answer would be misleading. The words are English.